Emotional Purity

An Affair of the Heart

Emotional Purity

An Affair of the Heart

Heather Arnel Paulsen, B.S.W.

Foreword by: Mark Misch

WINEPRESS WP PUBLISHING

Packaged by WinePress Publishing, PO Box 428, Enumclaw, WA 98022. The views expressed or implied in this work do not necessarily reflect those of WinePress Publishing. Ultimate design, content, and editorial accuracy of this work is the responsibility of the author.

Unless otherwise noted all Scriptures are taken from verses marked NASB are taken from the New American Standard Bible, © 1960, 1963, 1968, 1971, 1972, 1973, 1975, 1977 by The Lockman Foundation. Used by permission.

Scriptures marked NIV are taken from the Holy Bible, New International Version, Copyright © 1973, 1978, 1984 by the International Bible Society. Used by permission of Zondervan Publishing House. The "NIV" and "New International Version" trademarks are registered in the United States Patent and Trademark Office by International Bible Society.

ISBN 1-57921-340-5
Library of Congress Catalog Card Number: 00-110227

Cover photograph and author photograph by: Colleen Paulsen
Hair and make-up: Lesli Paulsen

To my faithful family:
Arne, Julie, Colleen, and Lesli.
Without your daily love and
honesty, this book would not exist.

Foreword

What is emotional purity? That's a good question. The term "emotional purity" was something I had never heard of until a few years ago.

Eleven years ago I asked Christ into my heart as my Lord and Savior. Today I am a single 28 year old teacher and coach at a Christian college in Missouri. I have been part of numerous Bible studies, church singles groups, have worked at numerous Christian sports camps, was a youth director for a church while in college and, as a competitive athlete, have traveled all over the United States and overseas with the help of the Lord. All in all, I have been exposed to different people, from many backgrounds and walks of life.

With all of my experiences I have come to realize that emotional purity is one of the single most unaddressed issues in Christian circles today. As a Christian, I am aware of what the term "physical purity" means and almost any Bible believing Christian can tell you what God's Word says when it comes to the topic of physical purity in relationships. But, emotional purity, what's that?

First off I want to say that in writing this book, Heather Paulsen has hit the nail on the head with a topic that many Christian singles in their 20's and 30's struggle with in today's society. Many Christian singles have close friendships, relationships with the opposite sex, that lack clarity and at times leave them confused as to how they are to respond to each other's words, actions and motives. Sure, there's been some great books written on dating, courtship, discerning God's will, etc., but never has this topic been expanded upon as *Emotional Purity: An Affair of the Heart* so clearly does.

I have known Heather since the fall of 1996. I was coaching and training in Denver, Colorado when a mutual friend introduced us. Actually I didn't get to know Heather that well until after we had both moved away from Denver. Shortly thereafter she had asked me about my thoughts (as well as other Christian singles) on the topic of "emotional purity" from the viewpoint of a young Christian single male. We had stayed in contact every few months through e-mails and phone calls.

When Heather returned home to Illinois after living in Denver the Lord laid it upon her heart to write this book based upon her personal experiences and that of many others, mine included. Over the course of the last three years, since Heather made the commitment to write this book, I have seen the need to study this topic grow more and more. I spend the majority of my time on college campuses and around young people dealing with the very topic of emotional purity on a daily basis.

I will be the first to say that in my own life, I have made mistakes in trying discern the motives behind someone's words, actions or intentions. I and many other good brothers and sisters in Christ I know wish we had gotten a book like this shortly after accepting Christ. It probably would've

Foreward

saved a lot of wasted time and energy in trying to sort through the complexity of male/female relationships in Christian circles.

I have also found this book to be interesting because as a male God calls me, and every other man, to a standard of leadership and responsibility in a relationship. Unfortunately in the last 2-3 decades, many mainline church denominations in our country have not even touched on this topic. The value and importance of Christ-centered relationships have not been taught thoroughly and most Christians learn first hand just like the secular society by trial and error, but not before someone's heart is hurt and usually that's just the beginning. This book addresses some of those very issues and many others backed by Scripture and God's words on the topic.

I would recommend this book to anyone no matter how old they are, whether they've been married and divorced or are still single or actively dating. It's really important stuff.

Heather, thanks again for the great job on writing this book and following through with what the Lord placed on your heart to do.

Mark Misch
January 2001
Bolivar, Missouri

Acknowledgements

To God Almighty—There are no words that fully express the deep sense of love and gratitude I have for You. May You receive all glory for this book.

To Norm Wakefield—Many, including me, thank you for teaching fathers to turn their hearts toward their children. Your ministry to my family has been a key to unlocking deeper levels of truth.

To Dr. S.M. Davis—Your teaching on the emotional fence we must protect has been the launching pad for this book and I thank you for your tenacity in teaching this message.

October 2000
Heather Arnel Paulsen
Lake Villa, Illinois

Table of Contents

Introduction

What prompted me to write this book on emotional purity? As a believer I desire purity in all areas of my life. I want to see God as number one in everything, and all I do should have His stamp of approval. I long for everyone to have this passion. We have come so far off the mark of emotional purity in our American culture that my heart cannot contain itself any more. Someone must make a bold stand for ultimate purity in this land and in our church. "Blessed are the pure in heart, for they shall see God" (Matt. 5:8).

My main objective for this book is to show through biblical examples the utmost importance of guarding your heart. Through studying the Scripture I have found that guarding your heart and your emotions is God's plan for the unmarried.

Five years ago I had a desire to be married, and it engulfed me mentally. I used to let my mind and heart wonder about the idea of being married to one of my "friends." My heart was unguarded and because of that, my

emotions were freely given away. After watching the heartache of many around me and experiencing my own, I saw a
pattern develop: emotional intimacy, no commitment, heartache.

Since then, as I prayed and searched the Word, God has
opened my eyes to some insight about the single life. The
plethora of new ideas brought me to a point where I can
honestly say, "For better days or for worse days, I accept
what God has for me as a single person. He will not keep
me unmarried a day longer than He plans. I will save my
emotions for God's plan and I will forgo the *games* singles
play." This declaration has allowed me freedom to fulfill
God's plan for my unmarried days.

Through the lives of fictional characters, the first chapter provides a reference point for the entire book. Tracy
and Luke's relationship represents the male-female interaction between many young Christians today. Their story
helps us begin to unravel the confusing aspects of
emotional purity.

The chapters that follow the story will examine their
relationship and the importance of guarding one's heart. I
will share some warning signs and give you tools that will
aid you in this journey to emotional purity.

Read this book with an open heart. Ask God to help
you throw aside any preconceived ideas on this subject.
Because it involves the heart of each of you, this topic is
difficult to fully explain. I ask you to search your heart.
God will help you realize that your heart must be pure in
all you do. As you read may your eyes clearly see God's
perfect plan.

November 2000
Heather Arnel Paulsen
Lake Villa, Illinois

1

Tracy and Luke

Tracy felt nervous as she waited for Emma to pick her up for Wednesday night fellowship. Since her move a week ago, she had already attended a local Bible church and immediately made a new friend.

As she curled her hair, picked out the right outfit and fussed over make-up, her heart said a thousand prayers. Tracy longed for a friend and, having had a great time at lunch on Sunday, she thought maybe Emma would fit the part. The doorbell rang. Six-thirty on the dot.

"Ready?" Emma asked.

Tracy grabbed her jacket. "Let's go!"

It didn't take long to reach the home where this gathering was taking place. Emma rang the bell, but before her finger released the bell the door opened to a tall guy with a welcoming smile. For a moment Tracy felt blown over by the very good-looking man in the doorway. She quickly regained her composure as she remembered that she was not there to meet "the one." He extended his hand toward them. "Hi. My name is Luke Hartman, and you?"

Emma confidently extended her hand. "Emma, nice to met you."

"Tracy Kass," Tracy said bashfully and slowly offered her hand to Luke.

Emma continued, "Are you new? I don't recall meeting you before?"

"Ye—" Before Luke could answer, a bubbly young girl embraced Emma and swept her into the living room, leaving Tracy alone with Luke.

"So, how long have you been attending this group?" Luke motioned for Tracy to enter into the house. Without giving her a chance to reply, he kept talking. "Your friend was right, I have never been here before. And can you believe they've got me answering the front door? I met some of these people Sunday at church and they invited me to this fellowship night. It seemed like a good mid-week pick-me-up." Luke stopped to catch his breath. "I'm sorry, I'm rattling on. What about you? Have you been here before?"

Tracy could not believe how totally comfortable Luke seemed. It made her feel more relaxed in this new environment. "No, this is also my first time attending one of these things. I just moved from Vermont and I don't know anyone except Emma, and we just met on Sunday."

"Oh, this is cool, someone new besides me. I just moved from Seattle. I got a job transfer and have only been here a week." He helped her take off her jacket as they walked into the living room together.

"Amazing, I have only been here a week as well." Tracy was somewhat shocked that she would meet someone with such a similar experience.

Throughout the evening they found themselves explaining over and over that they were not "together." By the end of the night it became a joke and Tracy and her new friend

Luke began acting as though they were together just to fool everyone.

Throughout the evening Tracy and Luke talked about their moves and the new paths that God was leading each of them on. He mentioned that he enjoyed tennis and she was excited to find someone else who liked the sport. Tracy had played on her college varsity team. Both eager to check out the local courts, they planned a tennis match for Saturday afternoon. Tracy could not believe how quickly the hours passed with singing, Bible study and fellowship. At nearly 11 o'clock, Emma announced that she needed to leave.

Luke opened his arms for a warm hug from Tracy. "I prayed that God would allow me to meet a friend, and I think He answered my prayers." Tracy felt a bit startled by this frank comment, but she accepted his hug.

"See you Saturday," she answered sweetly.

On the way home Tracy beamed with excitement, unable to erase her smile. Emma could see that Tracy and Luke had hit it off. She began firing questions. "Well, what do you think of Luke? You spent the night getting to know him. Is he good looking or what?!"

Tracy hadn't realized the attraction was so obvious. "He is really a nice guy and we just had so much in common. We're going out on Saturday."

"A date already! You go, girl!" Emma said, stunned.

Tracy was a bit taken aback. "I don't think it's a 'date' date. It's just two people going to play tennis."

"Whatever. I could see the way he looked at you, there is definitely something there," Emma replied. "You'd better call me on Saturday night and give me the details!"

That night Tracy couldn't sleep for thinking about the friendly people she had met and how awesome the fellowship had been. Her thoughts kept going back to her new friend, Luke. Her mind was set firm that she did not want to be hurt again.

- II -

Tracy spent Thursday and Friday evening on the tennis court, brushing up on her serve. With job hunting and the move she felt out of shape, and she did not want to make a fool of herself on Saturday. Her heart felt warm each time she remembered Luke's engaging embrace.

A good game of tennis was just what Tracy needed after a week at her new job. She felt surprised at how good Luke was. He gave her a run for her money. Afterward, they decided to grab a bite to eat.

Tracy felt very relaxed around Luke and wanted to know more about his walk with the Lord. While they munched on burgers and fries she asked, "When did you come to know Christ?"

"Well, I guess I always have known about Christ. My parents were awesome examples of Christ and when I was four I asked Him into my heart.

"During high school, guys from my Bible study and I started a weekly prayer meeting at our school. It's still strong and has seen over 200 kids come to know Jesus. Another growing experience I had was when I gave up a Thanksgiving at home with my parents to go on a mission trip to Africa." Once started on the subject, Luke seemed eager to keep talking.

"My love for the Lord grew even more in college. My freshman year I plugged into a Bible study with four other guys. We started a Christian fraternity at my mostly heathen college campus and it became one of the most respected fraternities. We were referred to on campus as the "God Squad."

Tracy chuckled. Luke went on, "Those buddies have become my closest friends and we always joke that when we get married our wives will also have to be best friends with each other. Tracy, you'd really like these guys. Okay enough about me, what about you?"

Tracy saw his depth of character as he shared his deep love for their Savior. Also, was that comment about his buddies a suggestion that she may develop a friendship with his pals? She brought her thoughts back to the conversation, and shifted in her seat. "Well, my testimony is not as . . . well, let's just say I have more baggage than you."

"For starters," Tracy began, "I was not brought up in a Christian environment. We always went to church, but it never meant anything. My folks did the best they could but in high school I began to rebel against everything and everybody. I . . . well, I walked on the wrong side of the road. As I look back, all I know is that I was trying to fill my heart with something, but God would not allow anything to satisfy me but Him.

"During my junior year of high school I was in a car accident with my boyfriend. We had been drinking and we hit a tree. Neither of us was injured but it brought me to the Lord. We broke up and I started going to church. When I went that time, I was seeking to find the truth, not just going because it was the thing to do. One Sunday the preacher talked about Christ being a part of your every moment, and that is what I wanted. That afternoon my new boyfriend and I accepted Christ. We tried to have a godly relationship and we were planning to go to the same college, a small Christian college about three hours from my home, but I got accepted and he didn't. We decided that if

God wanted us together then being at different colleges wouldn't matter. But as the summer went on, we felt ourselves being drawn in separate ways. We broke up right before school started.

"At college I had awesome roommates. The three of us prayed together all the time. They showed me what it meant to be forgiven and to forgive myself. I dated a guy in college and he was another key in guiding me into building a deeper relationship with God. We were planning on getting married, but you know how life goes.

"I see God's perfect plan in bringing me out here, so far away from him. I think I needed to be away from the whole situation. See, he's getting married next spring and the girl he is marrying is—or should I say was—a good friend of mine. I know that God has my husband picked out for me, I just need to wait on His wonderful timing."

Tracy amazed herself as she released her deepest feelings—and to a man! She carried on. "Well, God has used so many different people and situations to draw me into Him, and I am thankful that He's a big part of my life."

Tracy glanced down at her watch. "Wow! It's four o'clock." *Where have the hours gone?* she asked herself. She could not believe how much they had shared. She squirmed in her seat and felt it was time to go.

Happy to be home, Tracy swung open the door to her modest apartment. Before the door closed behind her she noticed the red light flashing on her answering machine. She hit the play button before she removed her sweater or dropped her tennis equipment.

"Hi, Tracy. This is Emma. I can hardly wait to hear what happened with you and Luke. It's late in the afternoon— are you are still out with him? Give me a call when you get in. I want to hear any juicy details of your day. I'm so happy for you!"

Tracy didn't lose the smile as she dialed her new friend's number. "Hi, Emma. It's Tracy," she said with a light bounce in her voice.

"Tracy, I've been waiting for your call. So what happened with your tennis date?"

Not wanting to embellish the day or indulge her friend too much, Tracy simply responded, "It was nice. We did a great deal of talking. He is a great guy, and who knows what will happen?"

Emma fired questions at Tracy: How did he this? How did he that? Tracy wanted to think about the day quietly, so she sweetly said goodbye and tiredly headed for the shower. Thinking about Luke brought on a mixture of emotions she had thought were buried after her last breakup. But maybe, Tracy felt, God had brought Luke into her life for a reason.

- III -

One week ran into the next, and before long Luke and Tracy's friendship developed a pattern. Sunday mornings brought them together at worship, followed with an afternoon of lunch and fun with the singles group. Neither missed the weekly Singles' Fellowship Night, and then there was the standing date for tennis and lunch on Saturday. Sunday, Wednesday, Saturday. Church, singles fun, tennis. Sunday spiritual bonding, Wednesday social bonding, and Saturday fitness bonding.

One night, as Tracy wrote in her journal, her thoughts poured out, *Father, You know my innermost thoughts and how much I do not want to have these feelings for Luke, but they are here. He loves You so much and that quality makes me so attracted to him. He strives to serve You and longs to love You more each day. What do I do with these feelings?* She was thankful Luke never overstepped physical boundaries; she knew this kept them pure. They were very close and the closeness was what she valued most in their friendship. As weeks turned into months, Tracy's mind often wandered . . . could this be the pure relationship she only dared to dream of secretly?

Friday nights had become one of her few free nights. Tracy used them to tackle life's menial chores. She'd fallen into the habit of picking up her cleaning, stopping at the mall or grocery store, then home to make her weekly call to her family and finally clean up her tiny apartment that she mostly neglected the rest of the week. But this particular Friday night her apartment would just have to understand her lack of attention.

On Wednesday night at Singles' Fellowship Emma had made Tracy promise to have a girls' night out. "It's been way too long since we've gotten together," she said. "I feel like we haven't talked in ages." Tracy agreed and they arranged to meet for dinner and a movie on Friday night.

Seated in a secluded booth, the pair had just ordered pizza when Emma blurted out, "So, tell me—what's going on with you and Luke?" Tracy had felt twinges of eagerness to indulge someone with the happy details of her friendship with Luke. Emma would be a perfect friend to affirm her feelings. Tracy began to talk as the waiter deposited their cokes, and as they finished the last slices of pizza she was telling Emma of her growing feelings toward Luke.

"Oh that's normal, Tracy. You two spend so much time together and he's a nice guy."

"But, Luke has never told me his intentions. What if he doesn't like me in that way? I mean, what if he just thinks of me as a good friend?" Tracy asked, hoping for reassurance.

"Tracy, do you talk on the phone every night?"

"Practically."

"Does he hug you hello and goodbye every time you see each other?"

"Yes."

"Does he treat any other girl in the singles group like you?"

"No."

"Doesn't he always give you that playful nudge when you are talking about your tennis matches?"

"Yes."

"Didn't he take you to his co-worker's birthday party?"

"Yes—Brice, the guy he led to Christ."

"Didn't he give you a nickname—Squeak or something?"

"Yes, Squeak, like the noise of my shoes when we play tennis."

"Well then, he has got to like you! All the signs are there."

Tracy's heart skipped. "You think so?"

"Yup."

That was what Tracy wanted to hear. She felt God confirming Luke's feelings toward her through this conversation.

The following Saturday's tennis match was a real workout for Tracy. She couldn't keep her mind on the game and ended up chasing balls all around the court. Exhausted and ready for a relaxing lunch, she fell into the cushioned booth and asked Luke to order "anything refreshing" for her. As she sipped on a large iced tea, Tracy began to share with Luke a conversation she'd had with Brice, Luke's co-worker, during the week.

"I was shocked when he asked me out. I mean, I hardly know him. We just met at his birthday party and I guess he felt comfortable asking me out. Well, he really isn't my type. I know you have just recently led him to the Lord and I praise God, but the last thing I need to deal with is a guy who is new in Christ. I need someone who is solid in the Lord," Tracy said with a nervous laugh as she wondered whether Luke was going to pick up the clue that she needed a man like him.

Only then did Tracy realize that she'd been twirling her first bite of salad around for several minutes while she chatted. Abruptly she took her first bite. She awaited a look of fear or disappointment in Luke's face at the thought of her dating someone else.

"His question really threw me off guard," Luke said as he dabbed his mouth with a napkin. "Brice asked me if he could ask you out. Now, why would he do that?"

Tracy's head bobbed up from her plate. "He asked you?"

"Yeah, isn't that crazy?" He responded with a partial laugh.

Tracy's mind whirled with uncertainty. *Did those guys discuss me over a coffee break? Did Luke mention any feelings he has for me to Brice? Luke must have told him it was okay to ask me! What's going on?* She unruffled her thoughts enough to counter, "Yeah, he is crazy,"

"Hey, let's get a movie and go back to my place!" Luke said abruptly as he stood up, grabbed the bill and paid.

At his home Luke popped in the video and sat down next to Tracy on the couch. At first she was nervous, but then Luke put his arm around her. "Just think, Squeak. If you had gone out with Brice tonight we wouldn't have had such a terrific time today."

"This is true," Tracy said as she snuggled effortlessly into his arm. She felt very secure there and briefly reflected that she was thankful Luke was being so cautious with her in regard to physical purity. Tracy couldn't remember a time in many months when she had felt such an overwhelming feeling of protection.

- **IV** -

Tracy felt homesick and confused. When time allowed, her thoughts would wander back to the stunning fall colors back east. She could only imagine the spectacular show they'd be putting on in her parents' well-manicured yard in New England. Envisioning these colors only intensified Tracy's loneliness. Thanksgiving away from her family— their traditional time for baking, taking a gift basket to a needy family and then the afternoon of feasting and football—threatened to be difficult for her. But Tracy was rather amazed that another little part of her was energized by thoughts of beginning new traditions. During one of those reflective moments, Tracy shared her homesickness with Luke by e-mail. She knew he would understand because he had been in Africa over the holidays when he was in high school.

On Saturday Luke asked Tracy what she had planned for Thanksgiving.

"Nothing, silly. I told you that in my e-mail." Tracy wondered where this conversation was headed.

"Well, I called my folks, and you know what? We have one extra chair at our Thanksgiving table. Would you like to fill it?" Luke asked.

Tracy's heart soared at the thought of meeting Luke's family. Her mind recklessly fired questions. *Could this mean something? What will I wear? Is there time to lose a few pounds? Will they like me? Will I meet his whole family? Does he want me to meet the folks before he takes our relationship*

to the next level? He must like me. Are his feelings developing
for me?*

The awkward pause of silence forced Tracy back to reality. She blurted out, "Yes, I would love to go!"

They made plans to leave a few days before Thanksgiving because Luke was asked to speak on Wednesday evening
for his old high school youth group. The next few days
were one big blur for Tracy. Finally, the time arrived, the
one event that had dominated her thoughts for way too
long.

As Luke pulled up and quickly packed Tracy's bags in
the flatbed of his truck, he gave a brief prayer for safe trav-
els and a holiday to remember. Off they went.

The next few hours filled Tracy with emotional highs.
"God is in control," they belted out along with Twila Paris
on the radio. Luke gave Tracy the lowdown on his parents
and siblings after they discussed Luke's topic for the youth
group the next evening. Tracy didn't even notice the re-
markable scenery zooming past her window as Luke painted
a vivid picture of his family's Christmas. Her full attention
was riveted on him as his story led to a mutual promise to
exchange Christmas gifts in one month. Tracy's whole world
seemed to be contained in the little Toyota truck as they
traveled down the road, each hour blending with the last.

Without warning, they arrived. As they pulled into the
driveway Tracy glanced at the clock and was stunned. *Where
have the hours gone?* she asked herself.

They left the luggage in the truck as Luke led the way
to the house. Any nervousness she felt as the door swung
open on this new world immediately melted as she soaked
in the warmth of his parents' greetings and hugs.

"We always enjoy getting to know Luke's friends," and
"so glad you could be with us for Thanksgiving," Audrey

and Jack blurted simultaneously. Tracy was overwhelmed with a sense of kindness and sincerity. Luke and his dad disappeared outside to unload the truck.

Luke's mom gently put her arm around Tracy, leading her into the kitchen. Only then did Tracy detect a great aroma. "I hope you like what's for dinner tonight," said Audrey. "I'm glad we have a few minutes to get acquainted before Sara arrives from work and Tommy gets home from school." Tracy smiled, as she remembered her feeling of thankfulness that they'd arrived early enough to allow for some family time that evening.

"Smells great, can't wait to meet your family." Tracy beamed. "What can I do to help"? Tracy instantly bonded with Luke's mom.

The smell of coffee woke Tracy the next morning. The house remained silent, so she quietly showered and dressed for the day. Scooping up her Bible, she headed downstairs and anticipated a few quiet moments in the overstuffed corduroy chair she had nestled in the night before. As her foot hit the last step, she spotted Audrey sitting in the very chair. Tracy stopped in her tracks when she noticed a Bible in Audrey's lap, and her head bowed. The praying woman's head gently turned as she realized her houseguest was present. She invited Tracy to join her, and that was the beginning of a nearly perfect day. An intimate breakfast with Audrey led to a day of running to the grocery store and then preparing side dishes for Thanksgiving with the women of the family. Dinner was full of pleasant conversation and stories of hilarious, embarrassing family moments.

As Luke and Tracy drove to his youth group engagement she realized they hadn't been alone since the previous day. Luke was deep in thought, rehearsing his talk. This freed Tracy to enjoy the ride in silence with her own

personal reflections. She loved that she could feel so connected to him without speaking a word.

The kids mobbed Luke before entering the church. He
looked at Tracy through the crowd and tried to communi-
cate, "I'm so sorry to leave you stranded alone in a strange
place, but . . . " Tracy actually enjoyed hanging out in the
background studying Luke's ease at relating to teens.

After an opening prayer with a round of praises, Luke
stood before the gym full of children on the edge of adult-
hood. As Tracy watched him connect with this group of
restless teens, she was falling in love with him. A passion
for Christ was all she wanted in a husband, and Luke filled
the bill. Tracy tried to focus, but her mind refused to grasp
one word of Luke's talk that evening. It chose rather to dwell
on a possible future with the man.

The ride home was completely opposite to the ride there.
Luke talked about how amazing the night had gone. Tracy
sat quietly, allowing Luke to fully unload all of his excitement.

Thanksgiving day activities intensified Tracy's feelings
for Audrey, Jack, Sara, Tommy, and, of course, Luke. She
was so engaged in Hartman family activity that she nearly
forgot to phone her own family with wishes for a happy
turkey day! During the day Tracy occasionally glanced
Luke's way with an enormous smile and sparkling eyes. She
wanted him to know this Thanksgiving was more than she
could have hoped for.

As Tracy rolled over and rubbed the sleep from her eyes,
she jolted into the reality that it was Sunday morning. Only
a few more hours until she'd be back in her little
apartment. As she lay there in a dreamy state, reflecting on
the last few days, Tracy realized she was not ready to say
good-bye to this family with whom she'd so quickly

cultivated a genuine love. She pondered the gentleness of Luke's mom and the carefree attitude of Tommy, who light-heartedly joined his brother in calling her Squeak. Each moment of the holiday held a certain level of importance in her heart. Not wanting to waste one minute of enjoyment with her new friends, Tracy bounded from the covers.

The whole family ate together and lingered over breakfast before heading off to church. Luke decided they should get an earlier start than they had planned, so Audrey offered to prepare a sack lunch of turkey sandwiches as the pair packed. As Tracy trudged down the stairs, she felt she was leaving a place she had grown to love.

Tracy hugged each member of the family goodbye. She hugged Audrey tightly, not wanting to let go. Audrey whispered in her ear, "Tracy, you're always welcome here. You're a lovely daughter in Christ and I know that the Lord has great plans for you." The words brought tears to Tracy's eyes; she never remembered hearing such sweet sentiments.

It seemed as if they'd just pulled into the now-familiar driveway, and now they were driving away, windows wide open as they waved until the family was out of sight. Tracy settled into her seat, overcome with a touch of melancholy. As they hit the freeway, Luke verbally began to review the past few days. Tracy's gloom slowly lifted as they laughed at Tommy's fumbled play in the family football game, and the disaster that had ended in rolling-on-the-floor laughter when Sara attempted to play beautician on Tracy's long hair. Luke suggested they break out the lunch as they settled in for the journey.

"You know, Squeak," Luke said, "I don't normally tell people this, but around the holidays I start thinking about having my own family and starting new family traditions.

Do you ever desire to start a family and your own traditions?"

"Sure I do. I can't wait to have my own family," she responded, wondering if he thought about establishing those family traditions with her. Their conversation remained on the topic of future goals and the dreams they each harbored. She was comforted by how much they had in common.

As they pulled up to Tracy's place, she said, "This was the first Thanksgiving that the main focus was family, and not mostly football. Your family took me in and treated me as a family member and I'm so thankful to you for inviting me."

"I'm glad you were able to come, Squeak. I could see many times over the weekend the joy that my family brought to you." Luke bent down and gave her a soft peck on her cheek. Their hug lasted a bit longer than usual.

- V -

For Christmas Luke gave Tracy a beautiful teal Bible with her initials, T.O.K., engraved in gold on the cover. Their telephone chats, which began as taking only a few minutes to confirm a time and place to meet, evolved into lengthy, soul-searching, into-the-night discussions. E-mails traveled back and forth as frequently and routinely as brushing their teeth.

Tracy went home for Christmas. Time away from Luke seemed like eternity. No matter how hard she tried to focus on her family and the gift of God's Son, her mind continually wandered back west, to the previous holiday's memories. Tracy loved to share with her sisters how important her relationship with Luke had become, but this only intensified her feelings of being away from him, and made her miss him even more.

Tracy and Luke

After the New Year, Tracy had a difficult time containing her emotions, and wondered if she could hold them in any longer. Her feelings for Luke had developed vigorously and she felt reasonably secure that he felt the same. Both agreed to forgo the customary tennis game for just this week to catch up on the sleep they had lost over the holidays, but they planned to meet for a bite to eat and catch up on each other's Christmas news.

Meeting at Tracy's favorite restaurant, she was thankful for the familiar atmosphere. "I'll have the usual," she muttered as she shifted uncontrollably in her seat.

"Do you have something on your mind, Squeak?" he asked. She was struck by his ability to read her like a book.

"Oh no, I'm just tired after the long holiday season," she said. That was not totally truthful, but she was using all her strength not to yell, "I love you!"

Trying to take the focus off her anxiety, Tracy strained to shift the conversation to how she had been able to share Christ's love with her family and how nice it was to be at home. As Luke related stories of his family's Christmas, Tracy's mind and heart raced frequently to the conversation she'd been planning in her mind since Thanksgiving. Lunch ended. Luke again paid the bill. They parted with a hug, and the long-intended conversation didn't pass Tracy's lips.

That night she called Emma to relieve some of her frustration. "Hi, this is Emma. I am not home right now, so please leave a message after the beep." The machine spewed. Tracy sighed, then drawled into the phone, "Emma, please call when you get home. I can't hold it in any more. I'll be up late, so call whenever, okay?"

That week Tracy felt nervous each time she saw Luke, her heart ached to tell him, but Emma constantly reassured

33

her that he needed to initiate taking the relationship to the next level.

The following Saturday Tracy ran errands and arrived early at the "Y," allowing a few moments to sit in the car and collect her thoughts. This was their first tennis match of the New Year and she was ready to work off some of her pent-up frustration, which grew larger every day she held back from speaking her true feelings to Luke.

Her thoughts rolled into a prayer, *"God, please help me today. I need your strength more every day. You have brought Luke into my life, and it would be an honor serving You with him. Let Your will be done and please help me accept it in Your time—which I'd really like to be soon, but I know Your time will be right. Just help me, Lord. I feel so mixed up."* Her mind whirled out of control. She grabbed her bag and headed inside to exercise away a bit of her anxiety.

She was picking up the key to the indoor court when she heard Luke's familiar voice from behind. "Hey, Squeak, did you get court number one?"

Hearing Luke's voice put a smile and glow on her face. As she answered she turned to face him. "Yes, I got . . ." Tracy's smile faded fast as she choked, and raised her hand to cover her gasping mouth. What she saw did not register in her brain. She felt her face turn pale and she wanted to run.

Luke stood there holding hands with another girl. Tracy choked again, which helped conceal the tears she felt well up uncontrollably.

"Squeak, are you all right?" Luke asked as he gently patted her back. "Yes, yes, I'll be fine," she muttered, wishing her Nikes would take over and carry her far, far away—away from this new girl who appeared to be in Luke's life.

"Tracy, I want you to meet my new girlfriend, Chrissy,"
Luke said. "Chrissy, this is Tracy, my great friend, the one I
told you so much about. She's been like a sister to me since
I moved here." He said as he curled his arm around Tracy's
drooped shoulder.

Good friend, Tracy thought. *That is all I am to you? "Like
a sister!" Oh, God, help me.* Tracy looked for a swift way out
of this situation.

"Nice to meet you," Tracy stammered, using all the
strength she had to be polite.

"Me too, Luke has told me so much about you. I feel
like I've known you as long as he has," Chrissy said.

"I thought you two could rotate each round," Luke suggested. "Got the key? Let's go!"

Tracy gracefully excused herself, making her way back
to the locker room under the pretense of forgetting her hair
scrunchy. "You two get started. I'll be right there." Inside
the locker room Tracy found the bench farthest from the
door, sat down and began to weep as shock turned into
reality.

*What am I going to do? I can't stay in here and cry all day.
He doesn't care for me at all like I do for him. What have I
gotten myself into!* She splashed her face with cold water.
"Lord, help. I need You now more than ever." Head held
high, but with lead in the pit of her stomach, Tracy headed
for the court with the navy blue scrunchy around her wrist.

"Hey, Squeak, it's your turn," Luke called as she trotted
onto the court. Each swing of the racket represented a blow
to her heart. Chrissy sat on the sidelines and watched. Tracy
had no competitive spirit. Luke swiftly won each match,
which answered Tracy's prayer for an quick end to this pain.
Her head already pounded with a headache that intensified

with each high-five between the flirting pair. She just wanted to be home in her safe apartment, far away from this scene.

Tracy fought back tears while driving and was happy to be safe in her cozy apartment. Falling into her chair, she let the tears overflow, then picked up the phone and called Emma for some comfort.

"Emma, he brought his *girlfriend* today!"

"What? Wait—who? Luke brought his girlfriend to tennis? You have got to be kidding!" Emma sounded stunned.

"No, they were walking hand in hand. He 'rotated us' each round. What was I thinking? He never liked me. See, he started this Bible study at work and she started coming and last week she accepted Christ as her Savior. And to top it off he introduced me to her as his 'great friend—like a sister.' I was so humiliated." Tracy became more irritated with each sentence.

Emma tried to help. "Tracy, he led you on! He treated you so different than anyone else in the group. He's such a jerk! You have every right to be mad at him. What are you going to do?"

Tracy thought. "I don't know. I'm sure we won't spend so much time together now that he has a girlfriend—who, by the way, is very perky and cute. Ugh! I thought I wasn't going to let this happen to me again. Argh! We weren't physical at all and we had such a solid base of friendship. I am just so confused. We were great friends." Tracy pulled the last tissue from the box.

"Let's do lunch tomorrow. Maybe that will help?" Emma suggested.

"I don't think so. I need some time alone. Thanks anyway. You've been a great friend." Tracy said.

Thought Questions:
1. Which character, Tracy, Luke, Emma or Chrissy, did you most relate to and why?
2. Before Chrissy came into the picture, what was your impression of Tracy and Luke's friendship?
3. If you were writing Tracy and Luke's next phone conversation, what would they say?

2

Emotional Intimacy

Tracy and Luke will never be as close as they were in the past. How did they fall into the common traps so frequently repeated by singles? Let's uncover some possible answers to this question and illustrate the thread that holds these problems together. Then we will look at ways to avoid the emotional intimacy trap.

In a society where friendships between men and women are common, accepted and encouraged, why do we have so many broken hearts over friends? Why are emotions spent and hearts bonded, as we saw with Tracy and Luke, with little or no thought that there could be another path?

We must re-sensitize ourselves to the importance of guarding our hearts from the "just friends" battle wounds that we saw in Tracy. What was the core mistake this fictional couple made? Maybe you related to either Tracy or Luke in a personal way. Once these commonly misplaced affections are defined, you will perhaps be better prepared to assess situations that you or others may be experiencing.

Everyone understands physical intimacy. We call it by many names: petting, making love, having sex, making out—the list is endless. Emotional intimacy is just as important, but what names do we have for that? We have very few, if any, euphemisms for emotional intimacy. Maybe if we know what emotional intimacy is and how valuable it can be, we would begin to give it new names.

How many of us have heard, "Wait until you are married to 'go all the way'"? Chances are, if you have spent any time at church on Sunday you have heard this biblical command repeatedly. We are told that our bodies are the Lord's temple (1 Cor. 3:16) and that we are not to defile them with fornication (Rom. 13:13), which is illicit sex. This is wonderful biblical truth. When we take the step into marriage God plans for us to be pure in body (Heb. 13:4). We will see that God's plan is for us to wait until marriage before "going all the way" emotionally as well.

The American Heritage Dictionary defines emotions as "Agitation of the passions of sensibilities. A strong complex feeling."

It defines intimate as "Marked by a close acquaintance or familiarity. Very personal or private. A close friend or confidant."

Therefore, emotional intimacy would be a close, private relationship that would invoke strong feelings, passions, and the senses. You have had an emotional closeness with another person—a brother or sister, friend, co-worker, mate, or parent. Think about Tracy and Luke for a moment. How emotionally intimate were they? Their hearts were connected and they shared a deep bond. They had a strong, private, personal relationship that stirred up feelings. Tracy and Luke were emotionally intimate without ever defining that intimacy.

Because of this unspoken bond Tracy was confused about where she fit into Luke's life. Was she his girlfriend, or just his friend? Luke never clearly defined his feelings for Tracy, which left her wondering. When the relationship is not clearly defined you will be left playing the assumption game. Someone will be left wondering, when there is no clarity or stated expectation in a guy-and-girl relationship. This point is critical in understanding the danger of flirting with emotional intimacy before a commitment. It's just as dangerous as flirting with physical intimacy.

Let me explain. I have a few male friends. One in particular has been like a brother to me. Now, you may ask how we managed to not step over the lines of emotional intimacy. Simple. When I first met Bob we were up front about our feelings. It was clear on both sides that we were just going to be friends. We defined our relationship from the beginning. We treated each other as brother and sister, never expecting more than a friendship. Most of the time when we did things together my sisters, parents, or friends joined us. There was rarely a need for one-on-one time. As this developed, over time I came to consider him a brother. I had the honor of being a bridesmaid at his wedding and it felt as though my brother were getting married. I will be honest and admit that he is one of only a handful of guys of whom I have not ever—not even once—wondered, "Could he be the one?" This open honesty was the key in maintaining a brother/sister relationship. We never had to wonder about the other one; we never had unmet expectations. It is a beautiful friendship between a guy and girl.

Contrast that with another male friend I had. We worked together and developed a close friendship. The two of us shared dreams, goals, struggles, and frustrations. But we never talked about "us." Not knowing where I stood in his life left me playing the assumption game. My heart ran ahead of my head, and before long I planned our wedding. To my disappointment our relationship never went past the intimate friendship stage. This caused me to re-evaluate the way I handle male friendships.

When a relationship has emotional intimacy without a clear explanation or definition of the friendship, one or both people involved can be left with unnecessary scars. Christian men and women must avoid taking any unnecessary baggage into marriage.

Most of you reading this would agree that the church is the bride of Jesus. Marriage here on earth is established by God to mirror our relationship with Him.

Ephesians 5:22-32 says,

> Wives, be subject to your own husbands, as to the Lord. For the husband is the head of the wife, as Christ is also the head of the church, He Himself being the Savior of the body. But as the church is subject to Christ, so also the wives ought to be to their husbands in everything. Husbands, love your wives, just as Christ also loves the church and gave Himself up for her, so that He might sanctify her, having cleansed her by the washing of water with the word, that He might present to Himself the church in all her glory, having no spot or wrinkle or any such thing but that she would be holy and blameless. So husbands ought to love their own wives as their own bodies. He who loves his own wife loves himself; for no one ever hated his own flesh, but nourishes and cherishes it, just as Christ also does the church, because we are members of His body. For this reason a man shall leave his father and mother and shall be joined to his wife, and the two shall become one flesh. This mystery is great; but I am speaking with reference to Christ and the church.

This passage lays a crucial foundation for marriage. Let's take a closer look at our relationship with Christ. Before you commit your life to Christ, how intimate does God allow you to be with Him? Not at all! No commitment, no intimacy. No stated intention to Him, no intimate, Spirit-filled bond between you and God. Yes, God reveals Himself to you, but there is no "drawing near to the throne of grace," or "entering His rest," as we read about in Hebrews 4, without clearly stated intentions.

Commitment produces intimate relationships, in the God-given order. The order God established is not an intimate relationship *then* commitment. God shows Himself to you in different ways and allows you to choose Him. Before there is a solid commitment you do not enter into the Holy of holies, into the most sacred dwelling place with our Savior, into communion with His Spirit. You are not intimate with Him until that most significant step is taken: commitment. John 1:12 says, "But as many as received Him, to them He gave the right to become children of God, even to those who believe in His name." This change happens when we receive Him. It requires a commitment to rearranging our attitudes, desires, and motives to please Him. If you don't receive Him, you don't have an intimate relationship.

Since our marriage on earth should mirror the relationship with Christ, then there should be no intimate relationship without a commitment. Yes, that's right, no intimacy! This would also include physical and spiritual, not only emotional. Pastors and parents are quick to tell us to not go "too far" physically, but the core of physical intimacy begins with emotional intimacy. If we can fully understand the importance of having emotional purity before marriage, being physically pure will fall into its proper place. When the emotional wall in a relationship between a male and female breaks down, then it's hard—if not impossible—to prevent the breakdown of the physical wall. When people become emotionally intimate, physical intimacy is hard to prevent.

Mike Farris stated this in an article posted on Crosswalk.com Inc. "If a young person starts 'falling in love' at 13 or 14 years old, emotional commitments are made and inevitably broken. Pieces of one's heart are given away. After a while, emotional entanglements lead to physical activities. So-called minor activities at first. The activities get more and more intimate as the months and years drag on. After one has been a part of the dating scene for three, four, or five years, the natural physical response to romantic love—sexual intercourse—is tantamount to inevitable." Emotional intimacy will bring about physical intimacy.

Emotional intimacy is the kind of closeness and familiarity that stirs feelings and senses that promote a bond, a union that God reserves for the marriage relationship. "Marriage is to be held in honor among all" (Heb. 13:4a). Once we make a solid commitment and speak the marriage vows, we are free to experience intimacy on all levels: physical, emotional, and spiritual. When we commit our life to Christ it frees us to have a deep, emotional connection to the pulse and heart of God. It is impossible to have that connection before the commitment.

Hebrews 10:19-22 declares,

> Therefore, brethren, since we have confidence to enter the holy place by the blood of Jesus, by a new and living way which He inaugurated for us through the veil, that is, His flesh, and since we have a great priest over the house of God, let us draw near with a sincere heart in full assurance of faith, having our hearts sprinkled clean from an evil conscience and our bodies washed with pure water.

So we can see that only after we commit to Christ can we enter with confidence into, and enjoy the benefits of, a committed relationship with God.

Perhaps you're asking, "How will I ever know who is Mr. or Miss Right if I never get to really know anyone?" Or, maybe you just can't picture a way out of the intimate friendship you're involved in without hurting the other person enormously. How do you define your current relationship? What is your or your friend's intention with this relationship? Take some time to process these thoughts on emotional intimacy and in a later chapter we'll go a bit deeper into this multi-layered topic. You may be surprised at the freedom you'll experience when you are guarded from emotional intimacy before its appropriate time.

Thought Questions:
1. In your words how would you describe emotional intimacy?
2. Reread Ephesians 5:22-32, on page 42, how is this passage critical for laying a solid foundation for a God honoring marriage?
3. How important is it for you to follow the example of Christ and the church with regards to your marriage, even your dating? Explain.

3

Emotional Purity

Emotional purity. What comes to your mind when you hear that phrase? Emotional purity is a new concept for most of us, so it takes time to process. May God be a part of this process in a powerful way.

A contributing factor in the lack of understanding of emotional purity has to do with previous generations. In our American culture it seems as though old people hang out with old people, and young people hang out with young people. Generations do not mingle with each other and share ideas, thoughts, wisdom and feelings. This saddens my heart because there is much we can learn from each other.

Society today is different than it was in the past. Think back 100 years ago. Young men and women were not allowed to be free in their time together. They were generally chaperoned, and when they spent time together it was for the prospect of marriage. This guidance prevented emotional intimacy, and more people married. So, more people married when emotions were not doled out without some form of commitment. Interesting?

In *Critique of Modern Youth Ministry* Christopher Schlect examines why, as a society, we have this idea of "separation of generational influence." "Grandville Stanley Hall taught that each generation is, or should be, superior to the previous one, and therefore needs to break free from those which precede it," Schlect writes. G. Stanley Hall was a pupil of Horace Mann, an evolutionist. Years later we can see how that has played out in all spectrums of life. Most people believe they can gain more insight from their peers than from their old-fashioned parents or grandparents. Because most of us believe this idea that Hall presented, we have looked to our peers, and not our parents, for spiritual growth and emotional guidance.

John Dewey, a student of Hall, is considered to be the father of the modern public school system. Before Dewey, one-room schoolhouses—with children of all ages educated together—were the mode of education. This philosophy that promotes the younger generation as being superior to previous generations flowed right into the modern public school system. With that philosophy so integrated in the public school system, we can see how easily it has become a part of our thinking and culture. Knowing this, we can see how our Christian society has applied these beliefs. We see members of youth groups and singles groups looking to each other for spiritual growth and fellowship, when instead we need to look to our parents or older members of the body of Christ.

When my sister decided to stop attending the singles Bible study she received a telling comment from a friend. This well-meaning friend asked, "If you don't come to Bible study, how will you grow spiritually?"

In a recent article, Erik Johnson says it well:

Since we were told in the '60s to not "trust anyone over 30" generations have developed a vague distrust of one another. It is a subtle suspicion that has even infiltrated the church, where it is common for activities to be segregated according to age brackets.

This is unhealthy . . . If we examine biblical attitudes toward the generations, we discover that generational separation is squarely against the tenor of Scripture. ("Joining the Generations," *Discipleship Journal.*)

Throughout the Bible we see examples of the mixing of generations. Paul addresses this issue in his letter to Titus (chapter 2), where both older men and older women are to teach and exhort younger men and younger women in different areas. Older men are instructed to teach younger men to be sensible, be examples of good deeds, be pure in doctrine, dignified, and sound in speech. Younger women are taught to love their husbands, love their children, be sensible, pure, kind, workers at home, and subject to their husbands so that the word of God will not be dishonored. Older men and women of the church should teach these godly qualities. Do groups that have peer teachers follow this example?

When people separated themselves by gender, not age, less emotional intimacy took place. Men came calling to a young woman's house, not to be friends with her, but to look to her as a marriage partner. In times past and in other cultures, young people saw the importance of having guidance from their parents and grandparents in this decision. They were not proud in thinking they could do it on their own. And it is obvious that today's methods are not successful.

When we have this "free-for-all" method, emotions will be hurt and feelings stepped on. Friendship with the opposite sex is a delicate matter and should not be taken lightly. You may be playing with the heart of another person's future husband or wife.

Emotional purity remains protected when older guidance plays a role in our life. We are more protected from falling into an emotional trap. Was Tracy protected from emotional pain? Physically the two were pure, according to our Christian society. However, the line of emotional purity was violated and Tracy had the pain of another broken heart.

Do you know anyone who has had a similar experience? I'm sure you do. It may be you. I know it has been me. I allowed myself to become emotionally intimate with men and found myself falling for them only to be hurt when those feelings weren't returned and I'd hear those words, "Oh, we're just friends!"

It should not surprise us when older members of the body of Christ are unaware of this situation. When they were in their late teens and early twenties, many of them were married. Intimate male-female friendships were not freely accepted and it was understood that when you befriended a person of the opposite sex, it was for the pursuit of marriage.

How different would Tracy and Luke's relationship been had they "gotten to know each other" around family or older Christians? How would their situation differed had they both stated their expectations of their relationship upfront? Would they have been as prone to share emotions if there were older ears or eyes present? Would Tracy have even spent time with Luke?

At night, when I am tired, my emotional guard comes down and I start saying things I shouldn't. I have been known to "over share" to well-meaning male friends, and

my endless rambling builds emotional ties that do not belong.

This may sound old-fashioned and out-dated, but
before one-on-one dating was established many people took
a protective approach toward marriage, and the divorce rate
was much lower. There is something to be said for that old
tradition.

As a result of these cultural changes in relaxed male/
female relationships over the past 100 years the church has
filled itself with programs that actually encourage emotional
intimacy to take place. But I think it is beginning to back-
fire. I have seen firsthand how singles and youth groups
provide a stage for this emotional "strip tease" to take place.
Co-ed Bible studies are springing up all over. At these studies men and women are challenged to share deep spiritual
issues with one another. This can lead us down a path of
staleness with the Lord by taking our focus off of Him and
placing it on a group or a person in the group. Remember,
the devil can appear as an angel of light (2 Cor.11: 14), so it
may look "right" to have these close emotional relationships, but it may be a scheme of Satan to pull your focus off
of God.

Why do I say this? Men and women who share deeply
spiritual issues and gain an emotional and spiritual bond
with a peer group can become almost married to the group.
They cannot seem to go out on a Friday night without a
section of the group or the whole group. They find all they
need spiritually and emotionally within that group without a commitment to any one person.

Yes, I do mean all they need. Once a friend said to my
sister, "Why do I need to get married? I find all I need in
this singles group." These groups can meet not just
emotional and spiritual needs but also physical. Making
out, heavy petting, and, in some cases, casual sex is

common, tolerated and almost accepted. There is a promise of accountability in these groups, but I have rarely seen it occur.

The way I see it, when we separate into peer groups with men and women together we end up having "emotional fornication." Chew on that for a second. Repeat it out loud. *Emotional Fornication.* I remember the first time those words were put together in my thoughts. "What?" was my first response. "Yuck!" was my second. I didn't really care to define my past male friendships with such a disgusting thought. Consider this carefully and I think you'll agree that emotional fornication is an accurate definition for what goes on between people who share their hearts with someone who is not their spouse.

When a person fornicates before marriage we normally think of it in a sexual context. I'd like you to think about emotional fornication. Here's a word picture to help you understand where I'm coming from.

Imagine for a moment one of those huge lollipops, the kind that you buy at an amusement park candy store. Take off the wrapper and pass it around to ten people. Allow them to lick as much as they want. The left over is saved for the husband or wife, the rightful owner of the lollipop. Yuck! Who would want that? When we give pieces of ourselves emotionally and spiritually to ten different boy/girl friends what is left over for the rightful owner? Just the leftovers! The rightful owner is first God, then a mate of His choice. Keeping yourself emotionally pure is a gift that should be left wrapped and given to the rightful owner, your spouse.

When the lollipop is passed around for anyone to taste, it is not being kept pure. When we spread our hearts around and share deep emotional feelings with a boy/girl friend, or even a handful of boy/girl friends, we are robbing our future spouses of parts of our emotional selves. In a word— fornication. Being pure is the goal of the believer: "Blessed are the pure in heart for they shall see God" (Matt. 5:8).

Also, in Mark 7:20-23 Jesus tells us what defiles us:

That which proceeds out of the man, that is what defiles the man. For from within, out of the heart of men, proceeds the evil thoughts, fornications, thefts, murders, adulteries, deeds of coveting and wickedness, as well as deceit, sensuality, envy, slander, pride and foolishness. All these evil things proceed from within and defile the man.

It boils down to purity and holiness from within.

You might be trying to reason this out: "Sharing myself or my thoughts isn't bad, is it?" Or, "It's not hurting anyone, so what's the problem?" The problem is that when intimate ideas, secrets, or dreams are shared with wrong motives or unclear relationship boundaries, the heart feels the effects when those in unclear relationships break up or start dating someone else. A person feels rejected without ever being accepted as a "significant other." Tracy and Luke's relationship seemed harmless, but look what took place in Tracy's heart. When this scenario takes place repeatedly in a person's life, barriers are inevitably raised and the heart becomes protected with a massive, hardened wall. Imagine handing this shielded heart to a bride or groom. Let's hope this imaginary couple registered for a pickaxe and received it as a wedding gift. Because that's the tool they need to breakdown those walls. Definitely, this is one tool that shouldn't get lost in a corner of the basement or garage. Through the years this tool will become dull from the slow process of chipping through all the walls that have hardened to protect tender emotions. God in His power can make this process shorter and less painful when either or both partners look to God and trust Him to heal past hurts.

Now that I have learned to look to my parents, or in your case it may be an older Christian mentor, I find freedom to pursue God with all that I am. My parents went through the dating scene and experienced the negative consequences. Their insight is incredible. The 20-20 perspective from my folks gives me a safeguard from repeating generational mistakes.

Solomon repeats himself a number of times in the book of Proverbs: "Hear, my son, your father's instruction and do not forsake your mother's teaching" (1:8). "My son, give attention to my words, incline your ear to my sayings " (4:20). "My son, keep my words and treasure my commandments within you" (7:1). "Now therefore, my sons, listen to me and pay attention to the words of my mouth" (7:24).

Do you think that the wisest man in all of history should be listened to? He knew the importance of having godly parental guidance. Freedom comes with this protection, and my sensitive heart loves the safety net my parents provide. I know that in the long run I will be thankful I have not spent the last few years giving emotions to men that they do not rightfully own.

When you experience intimacy without commitment you are playing with the heart of a fellow brother or sister in Christ and will violate emotional purity. With so many singles receiving intimacy—spiritually, emotionally and physically—with members of the opposite sex, marriage is no longer special. When one has given away so many pieces along the way, the future husband or wife will not receive the whole heart. Would you feel like a special guest if someone invited you over for dinner and brought out impure, half eaten or regurgitated food? Let's see, your choices are Tuesday's meatloaf, Friday's chicken soup and three-day-old Chinese!

Emotional purity before marriage allows us the greatest opportunity to become emotionally intimate with our mate during marriage. Strive toward emotional purity and one day you will reap the rewards. God blesses those who desire purity and holiness.

Thought Questions:
1. Is emotional purity something you want for your life? If so, why?
2. How would an older mentor help you on your path towards marriage?
3. What helps you obtain and maintain emotional purity? What hinders it?

4

Defrauding

efrauding sounds like a courtroom term. Once we define defrauding, we will see that we need to avoid defrauding our brothers and sisters in Christ.

Enhanced Strong's Lexicon states that the word defraud comes from the Greek word *pleonekteo* (pleh-on-cek-thé-o), which means to have more, or to gain or take advantage of another, to overreach. *Pleonekteo* is derived from the Greek word *pleonektes* (pleh-on-ek´-tace), which means one eager to have more, especially what belongs to others.

Webster defines defraud as to swindle or cheat.

What does defrauding have to do with being friends? Basically, you defraud people when you use them, or cheat them of something they need to save for someone else. One could define it as teasing them with what they cannot have. When you play with the emotions or expectations of someone in which you do not expect to righteously satisfy, you are defrauding. You cannot righteously satisfy another person until you make a commitment.

The word clearly tells us to not defraud one another. 1 Thessalonians 4:3-6 states,

> For this is the will of God, your sanctification; that is, that you abstain from sexual immorality, that each of you know how to possess his own vessel in sanctification and honor, not in lustful passion, like the Gentiles, who do not know God; and that no man transgress and defraud his brother in the matter because the Lord is the avenger in all these things, just as we also told you before and solemnly warned you.

This passage continues the thought of sexual immorality and lustful passions by warning us to "not defraud" one's brother (or sister) in the matter. Why? "For God has not called us for the purpose of impurity, but in sanctification" (verse 7), or "For God did not call us to be impure, but to live a holy life."(NIV)

"So, he who rejects this is not rejecting man but the God who gives His Holy Spirit to you" (1 Thess. 4:8).

Also in Mark 10, in a dialog between Jesus and the rich young man, Jesus tells him in verse 19, "Do not defraud."

In our society, there is a common acceptance of defrauding one another in uncommitted, emotionally intimate friendships between men and women. We have become desensitized to the emotional purity of our friends. We defraud each other in this arena without even realizing what we are doing.

As we saw in the Greek, "defraud" derives from a word that means taking something that is not yours. What did Luke take from Tracy that was not his? He took parts of her heart and emotions. What did Tracy take from Luke? She took his time and energy he should have been using to build his family. Both of them took something that did not belong to them; they emotionally defrauded one another.

Tracy and Luke were connected emotionally and spiritually. They passed the point of no return. Tracy allowed herself to become attached to Luke with no solid evidence of his intentions. Once she became emotionally and spiritually involved with him, there was no way for her to leave the friendship without some bumps and bruises on her heart. "Watch over your heart with all diligence, for from it flow the springs of life" (Prov. 4:23).

How does defrauding occur during a simple dating relationship? Maybe this familiar example will shed some light on what I mean.

Guy and girl begin to date each other. They are in the stage of getting to know each other, so they spend a great deal of time together. Physical activity never reaches the point of intercourse, but they visit the edge once or twice. They spend the holidays with each other's families; they pray together about their relationship, while all along there is no talk of marriage. They have a very "normal" dating relationship. After spending a year getting to know each other with no commitment to the future, the guy realizes she is "the one" and decides to pop the question. She is overwhelmed with apprehension, says she's not ready to be committed and decides to "take a break from the relationship." They never do come back together and the guy has a broken heart, wondering if he will ever become that close to anyone again.

How did they use or defraud each other? Take a closer look at their relationship. They had emotional, spiritual, and physical intimacy without a solid commitment to protect them from the start. They had this intimacy with no long-term commitment: they defrauded each other. They took time, energy, and emotions from one another. They took parts of each other's heart that did not belong to them.

Let's go back to 1 Thessalonians 4:6, where Paul states, "...that no man transgress and defraud his brother in the matter, because the Lord is the avenger in all these things..."

The NIV says it this way: "And that in this matter no one should wrong his brother or take advantage of him." The matters he is talking about are in verses 3-5: "For this is the will of God, your sanctification; that is, that you abstain from sexual immorality, that each of you possess his own vessel in sanctification and honor, not in lustful passion, like the Gentiles who do not know God."

We see in verse 4 that God calls us to sanctification and honor. Sanctification is the act of purifying oneself, holding one's "vessel" in honor, respecting oneself. When one crosses lines into deep emotional and spiritual connections, one takes pieces of another's emotional and spiritual purity that need to be saved for that person's marriage partner. When you give your heart away you are giving what belongs to your future mate. Will you be able to present yourself whole-hearted at the wedding altar or have you left pieces of it with others? Christ came so that we may be presented before God as holy and blameless, beyond reproach. We, the church, (bride) are to strive toward *all* purity so that we may be presented before Christ (bridegroom) holy and blameless. We should reflect that in our earthly marriages.

Let's say you just bought a shiny new 4x4 oversized truck with all the extras. After leaving the lot you run some errands. When you are done shopping, you come out to your truck to discover that the Yugo next to you put a dent in your door. Not a large dent, just enough to scrape off some of the paint. If this happens too many times, it affects the value of the car. So, too, is the human heart. When a heart goes through nicks, bumps, scratches and bruises it loses the newness for the correct owner.

All too often Christian men and women emotionally defraud each other by asking for feelings with no obligation. They toy with commitment-free-relationships.

We need to be careful in all that we do. Women can defraud by the clothes we wear. Provocative clothes can steal the heart of a man. Men should learn to despise the Proverbs 7 woman about whom Solomon warns young men: "Do not let your heart turn aside to her ways, do not stray into her paths. For many are the victims she has cast down" (Prov. 7: 25-26a). When a woman dresses in a way that stirs a young man's heart her way, she may whet an appetite she has no business whetting.

A man's tender attention and smooth words can steal a girl's heart. However, the young girl in Song of Solomon requests repeatedly not to arouse or awake her love until she pleases. Men, when you treat a young lady as "special" you may be whetting her appetite for marriage.

We all can understand the beauty of saving our physical bodies for our mates. How much more wonderful if we saved our emotions as well.

When one avoids defrauding, blessings will follow. I tend to not spend one-on-one time with any guy. I am not emotionally available to every young man who comes along. I have not held a guy's hand in years, or had a deep emotional or spiritual conversaton with a male "friend." Now, let's imagine that I remain physically pure for my husband, but hold hands with other guys, spend one-on-one time with them and have deep emotional connections with good guy friends. What does that take away from my husband? My appreciation. Do you know how thankful I will be when I am able to share those common things with my spouse? Very thankful! I will praise God for allowing me to be alone with him, hold his hand, share all of my heart with him and have his arms around me. These experiences will be all so new to me. It will be an adventure to share it only with the man I will be married to for the rest of my life—could it get any better? Finding and maintaining emotional purity before marriage will greatly enhance your marriage and, my friends, that is true romance!

Even after marriage one will want to continue to strive towards this purity. Unfortunately, husbands and wives are committing emotional defrauding and emotional fornication with other people at work, at church, and even more so on the Internet. In doing research for this chapter, I found hundreds of postings from husbands and wives who discovered that their mates were a little too intimate with someone via the computer. When this problem struck close to home, I began to see the magnitude of this issue.

The following is a factual account of Nathan and Darla, long-time family friends. This story perfectly illustrates the gravity of emotional defrauding.

Nineteen years ago this couple married after dating in high school. They attended church regularly and, after eight years of trying unsuccessfully to have children of their own, they adopted two children. Darla was a stay-at-home mom and home schooled the children. Nathan was a hard-working provider for his family. When their children were young innocently Darla began to play Atari and Nintendo, then Sega. Over the years, this "harmless" pastime used up many hours during the day and going late into the night. This activity led to playing on-line role-playing games. Darla met a man on-line from another country. Her role-playing character had an on-line marriage with his character. This man is younger than she and their bond started as many on-line and person-to-person friendships do—very innocently.

Darla became more aloof. She was caught lying and began to pull away from many close friends. She was spending more and more time on-line chatting with this man. My sister, a trusted friend of hers, received a call from Darla. She told my sister that in the past few months she had started feeling sorry for Nathan. He knew about this guy in another country and Darla felt bad that he did not have "someone to talk to." So, Darla's simple solution was to introduce her husband to a woman on-line.

Within weeks Nathan visited his new computer friend, a soon-to-be-divorced, mother of two who lived just hours away. In less than two months, Nathan and Darla decided to divorce. The other woman and her children moved into the house with Darla, Nathan and their family. According to Darla, she's thankful her husband has "found someone," and they're reportedly happier than anyone could have imagined. This whole scenario is abhorrent. Yes, there's an obvious defrauding taking place.

Just recently, Dr. Laura Schlessinger hosted an hour-long TV show titled *When is an Affair an Affair?* This program dealt with committed couples who had emotional relationships with people other than their partners. Some of these led to physical relationships; others did not. Dr. Laura summarized her feelings on the matter:

> Anything that could lead to an affair also qualifies as part of the affair. . . . It should be clear to you that relationships outside of marriage, whether by use of the Internet or by some other means of spending time together, are improper and a form of adultery no matter what you want to call it.
>
> Intimacy is not just about physical encounters. When someone shares inner feelings, secrets, desires, flirts or flatters, or even places himself or herself in a compromising situation, you are being intimate. The final analysis: all forms of intimacy should be reserved for the marital relationship or else you are taking something away. Something that belongs to the spouse and giving it to someone else. That wasn't what the vows were about.
>
> The ultimate deterrent to all of this is a strong set of moral values, rules, and standards. These keep you from

even taking the first step. Because, for sure if you don't take that first step, you won't be there to take that final fatal step.

Also, Dr. Laura conducted a web poll that day. The question: "Should an emotional, but non-physical relationship be considered an affair?" The results back up the thesis of this book: 72 percent said yes; 28 percent said no.

Emotions. It's emotions! We are all beginning to see the role of emotions. Darla formed an emotional connection with this young man. She defrauded him and vice versa. Do you see it? Satan saw the weakness and used it to his advantage. It's still hard for me to believe that a strong emotional attachment, the object sight unseen, became the sole basis for Darla's willingness to throw away her marriage and family. It's been over a year since she met her on-line friend, and Darla spent the holidays with this man—not even returning for Christmas. How sad! Emotions, can they be trusted? Would you say Darla committed emotional defrauding, or shall I say adultery?

For those who think that this emotional purity and defrauding stuff is a big joke, please rethink your position. Darla herself once held that opinion, telling my sister that she didn't understand why anyone would "save" herself emotionally for marriage. Well, Satan used that lack of understanding in Darla to destroy friendships, trust, children's lives, a marriage, a family, and a relationship with God.

Emotional defrauding can pull any one of us away from the Lord. All types of relationships—innocent friendships or even Darla and her e-mail buddy—can have devastating effects on one's marriage and children, when people do not remain emotionally pure.

Why did the emotional relationship between Tracy and Luke pull the focus away from God? Were they concerned with seeking what is best for the other, or were there selfish motives behind the friendship? Could Darla or Tracy really see what they were wanting from these friendships? The answers to these difficult questions deal with the heart of people. True motives of their heart are laid bare with honest examination. Satisfying a friend's emotional needs may be done with pure motives, but may not be best for the other person. Only God allows you to meet someone's emotional needs.

Married or single, we must avoid defrauding, taking something that does not belong to you. He wants us to obey this commandment to protect us. He wants to show you how good purity feels.

Thought Questions:
1. In your own words, describe emotional defrauding.
2. What are ways you can prevent emotionally defrauding someone?
3. Why is an emotional, but non-physical relationship an affair?

The Female Heart

God created women with a heart more sensitive and emotional than men. How shall this heart be nurtured and protected? Titus 2:4–5 instructs older women to encourage younger women to love their husbands and children. The Greek word for love here is *phileo*. Most of the time when you see the word love, the Greek word is *agape*. *Agape* means a love that earnestly desires and wants the best for another. *Phileo*, the love a wife is to have for her husband, means friendship, an emotional attachment type of love. This is where we get Philadelphia, "City of Brotherly Love."

I have yet to meet a woman who, when totally honest with herself, won't admit she has a tender heart. However, with years of being vulnerable and then hurt, her heart has become calloused. God's plan when He made Eve was to give women tender hearts. He made this heart desire love and to love. He made women emotional and caring.

Men need to know that a woman is an emotional person and, unlike them, can become emotionally connected.

A woman's ability to emotionally connect quickly is heart glue for her marriage, not her male friendships.

This reminds me of a story. A close friend of mine, Connie, befriended an older Christian man, Joel. Joel flirted with her by tugging on her hair, giving her a nickname, and spending countless hours with her. He was never upfront with how he felt, and her heart fell for him even though she knew this was not how she wanted her marriage to begin. Connie eventually confronted Joel and he gave the all-familiar brush off, "Oh, no we're just friends." Their relationship took away emotional glue for her marriage.

Capturing a girl's heart, attention, and loyalty before a man knows how he feels about her can be compared to stealing a hot rod to take out on a joy ride. Would one risk being caught with a stolen car, then paying the consequences, for a momentary cheap thrill? Those pride-filled, microscopic seconds in time, which may have been full of excitement and adventure, may reap a lifetime of paying the price. This is exactly what happens when you toy with someone's emotions without commitment. The joy ride may have been an emotionally satisfying, ego-stroking, and self-pleasing experience, but it could hurt all parties involved.

A woman never forgets her "first love." Many older women can tell you specific details about her first love, first date, first kiss, etc. My mom and dad went to a Valentine's party a few years back. They watched a "newlywed" type of game with people married 40-plus years. When the men were asked what their wives wore on their first date most of them made it up, but the women remembered everything, right down to the bobby socks and poodle skirts. Not only did they remember the event, but the details surrounding these emotional attachments. There was a twinkle in the men's eyes as their wives were thinking back on a time when they experienced that emotional rush of infatuation.

God created women with different emotional needs than men. If we were created alike then our commandments would be identical. Notice how the commandments are written:

"*Husbands* likewise live with your wives in an understanding way" (1 Pet. 3:7).

"*Husbands* love (*agape*) your wives, just as Christ loves the church" (Eph. 5:25).

"Older *women* . . . encourage younger women to love (*philo*) their husbands" (Titus 2:4,5).

"*Wives*, be subject to your husbands, as is fitting in the Lord" (Col. 3:18).

Men's inspired command is to love their wives and be understanding with them so as not to hinder their prayers (1 Pet. 3:7). Women need to learn to be subject to their husbands and let "the hidden person of the heart, with the imperishable quality of a gentle and quiet spirit" (1 Pet. 3:4) guide their words, thoughts, and actions.

Since we are created different, single men and women need to take responsibility to how the other person will react to the attention they are giving. One does not want to cause a fellow brother or sister in Christ to stumble, stray, or lose their undivided focus on God.

What if Luke had been aware that creating an environment for Tracy to share so openly caused her to be more focused on their friendship then her relationship with God? Would he have been more cautious? If he had seen Tracy as a potential marriage partner how would he have treated her differently? If Tracy had not given herself emotionally to Luke, it's possible she would have looked old-fashioned. I know people who think I have fallen off my rocker because I am not emotionally available to any guy who comes along. How sad that we look at the ways of the past and think of them as out-dated, when in reality our modern ways of thinking open the door to all kinds of hurts. My sisters and I have been teased because of our desire to remain emotionally pure. We have been called Puritans and "peculiar." Well, what's so wrong with being called either of those? All Christians should strive to attain purity in all areas of their life.

As single people, we need to consider the chances that we may be dealing with another person's future spouse. Would you like to know that your future mate is giving him or herself emotionally and spiritually to another? I would venture to say that none of us would like that much. If Luke marries his new girlfriend, what about the connection he had with Tracy? His wife will always know about the deep bond they shared. All this could have been easily avoided had Luke not pursued a friendship with Tracy unless he was very clear with his intentions.

Luke did not exactly understand what Tracy was going through; nor should he. Maybe he had a clue of what she was feeling, but he was enjoying the stroking of his male ego. After all, Tracy was beautiful and paid him attention. Tracy also gained selfish pleasures from the relationship, feeling protected and cared for. Because they walked this fine line of emotional free-for-all, Luke's "out" was simply to say, "I just don't understand women." I agree totally. But he's not required to understand *women*, but *one woman*. Remember the Bible says, "Live with your wife in an understanding way" (1 Pet. 3:7). Peter's not saying, "Live with *women* in an understanding way!"

Another way of protecting a woman's heart is through the loving care of her father. I realize this cannot happen in all cases, but when you understand the protection a father can give, you will quickly realize you can be protected from emotional hurt.

Learning about the heart of a woman could take a life-time. God created male and female to represent His whole being. He is the God of understanding and can open our eyes to purity in all areas.

Thought Questions:
1. How does one care for the heart of a woman?
2. Why is it important for a woman to marry her first love?
3. If you looked at all your single friends as someone else's mate, would you treat them any different? Why?

6

Just Friends

Can you be "just friends"? How does friendship play out in dating, courtship, and marriage with a biblical perspective? As I have pointed out, God created husband/wife relationships here on earth to help us see more of His love. Marriage should be a taste of heaven. Allowing God to show us healthy boundaries in relationships is a key to maintaining emotional purity.

Reexamine Tracy and Luke's friendship applying this knowledge of commitment first then emotional intimacy. If Tracy and Luke had been more careful with handing out emotions there would have been a completely different outcome. Tracy guessed, wondered and imagined what Luke thought. A friendship becomes dangerous at this point. Having no idea what a friend thinks creates a vacuum for you to fill with your own ideas and goals for the friendship.

I know this concept is weird. Trust me, I have had to rethink many of my own male friendships, and the world is not helping. Just the other day I was listening to a Christian radio program about dating and physical purity before marriage. The young man talking almost hit the target. Then in so many words he said, "A single person needs to have lots of male/female relationships in order to know how to relate to the opposite sex." Lost me there! See when we view guy/girl relationships through the model of Christ and the Church, we see no intimate friendship stage.

Do I think it is wrong to have male/female friendships? Of course not! I have a few myself. However, the danger is the emotional "free-for-all" that Christian singles play around with. Emotions are given, tossed about and sometimes stolen without a cost.

Susan Nikaido put it well recently in *New Man Magazine*: "If a man *tells* a woman he just wants to 'be friends' but he *treats* her like it's more than a friendship, she will believe his behavior instead of his words." With the free-for-all we have, this scenario happens over and over in Christian singles groups.

My guy friends defined our relationship. There is no wondering if any of them is "the one." With these boundaries we are free to enjoy each other's fellowship as brother and sister in the Lord.

I have met some "marriageable" men and this "where do we stand?" conversation has not occurred. What is my response? Knowing full well that God is in control, I treat these men as I would anyone. As our relationships currently stand they will be someone else's husband. I do not pay special attention to them and I keep my thoughts captive to Jesus Christ. I must control my actions and thoughts because, at this point, there is no commitment or hope of a life-long partnership with any one of them. This takes work, my friend, but in the end everyone will be better off.

I will say there is a level of emotional ties in these friendships, because with any friend there would be some connection. The brother/sister relationship is an excellent guide for me in these friendships. When there is no commitment or hope of a long-term future with them, the emotions stay in their proper place because of the boundaries. Now ideally, when lines are clearly drawn both parties are free to have a relationship that is not focused on the "what ifs" but on the now. You can have this type of relationship without the "defining-the-relationship" conversation. It will take self-control, many prayers, and a few reality checks, but it will save heart pain in the end. As in actual brother and sister relationships, there is never that guesswork.

For men and women the dilemma of understanding each other is centuries old. It seems one gender is always trying to understand the other, but to no avail. So much confusion still occurs. I am no expert on men but, having grown up in a family with two older sisters, I would say I'm an expert on women. The three of us have spent hours searching our own hearts, and we have closely examined all the weird things we do.

Tracy would fit perfectly into our household. She is emotional, sensitive, and has a fragile female heart. Tracy mentally envisioned herself married to Luke, fitting right into his family, experiencing the protection of a strong spiritual leader, and enjoying a close friendship-leading-to-marriage relationship, when in reality they were just friends, nothing more, nothing less.

We aren't really sure how Luke viewed Tracy, but he enjoyed his newfound friend, not giving much thought to his future with her. Chances are he saw this as a perfectly normal, healthy, 21st-century, godly friendship.

Actually, most of you saw this as a normal friendship between a brother and sister in Christ. Tracy and Luke enjoyed each other's company while remaining physically pure. But something went wrong. This friendship took a turn for the worse.

Keep in mind the picture God paints when He stated that Christ is the bridegroom and the church is the bride. God wants the relationship between a husband and wife to mirror the relationship between Christ and the church. Since marriage begins at the commitment level, we need to line up friendship, dating, courtship, engagement, and marriage with God's depiction.

Many of you would say that friendship is important in marriage and I would wholeheartedly agree, but are you an *intimate* friend with Christ before you make a commitment? No! You grow into a deeply intimate friendship with Christ after you make a commitment. Why do we allow ourselves to think God would be pleased with dating, friendships, courtships, or marriages here on earth looking different than His design for our walk with Him? God does not play games. He does not tease you with emotional highs and lows to draw you to Him. He does not befriend you to leave you at an emotional "low" while He goes on to the next emotional "high" with another "friend." He asks for a solid commitment and does not take a halfhearted vow.

Guy/girl platonic relationships need to be re-examined. We must scrutinize what we are doing and see if it fits into God's plan for friendship and marriage. Many singles walk around with battle scars—emotional wounds created by undefined intimate friendships. There is a proper place for platonic relationships, and we must find that place in order to guard our hearts.

Joshua Harris examines male/female friendships in his book *I Kissed Dating Goodbye*:

"Being just friends with members of the opposite sex doesn't just happen by accident. We have to fight for and guard our friendships. Like magnets, men and women are designed to attract each other. But until we're ready to be 'stuck for life,' we need to avoid premature intimacy."

With God's plan for dating, courtship, engagement, and marriage we need to take a step back and look at the big picture. Have you ever had the chance to visit the Rocky Mountains? They are spectacular. They go on for miles and miles. I had the opportunity to live in Denver for a year and I developed a deep love for the mountains. Throughout the year I saw the mountains in many different perspectives. When you take the cog railway up to the top of Pike's Peak, along the way all you see is rocks, boulders, a cottage, and a lovely lake. You don't see the full view of the mountains. When you reach the top, the sight is breathtaking, you can see for hundreds of miles. From the top the picture of the Rocky Mountains is grander than the views on the ride up. Let's not focus on the rocks without looking at the bigger picture. God's ways are always better than what we could do for ourselves. They may require more patience, but in the long run they prove to be amazing!

Thought Questions:
1. What are your thoughts on male/female friendships?
2. How would you describe a godly brother and sister in Christ friendship?
3. Examine your current friendships, how do they line up to God's Word?

7

Commitment Equals Protection

What is the core of emotional purity before a commitment? Think about areas of your life where you make commitments. When you obtain a mortgage you make a payback commitment before the banks lends you the money. Your commitment protects the bank. When you join a fitness club, you make a commitment to pay the dues. Your commitment protects the club. Things come with commitment in life. In order to enjoy a house, new car, or a satisfying workout you have to make a commitment.

Have you ever worked on a group project in which one member of the group does the bare minimum? What a frustrating situation. It's like pulling teeth to get this member to complete his or her fair share of the project. Then, when you turn in the project, the slacker receives the same grade as those who worked diligently. The slacker receives the benefits of the grade, but never made a commitment to the project. Just like the project slacker, the relationship slacker will seemingly benefit at the expense of others.

When Mary found out that she was pregnant, Joseph was going to "send her away secretly" (Matt. 1:19). The

New International Version states, "His mother Mary was pledged to be married to Joseph . . . [he] did not want to expose her to public disgrace, he had in mind to divorce her quietly" (Matt. 1:18,19). How committed were they?

They were committed to the point that divorce was the way of ending their relationship. We never hear of them "dating" or "seeing if they are the right ones for each other." It seems as though they jumped in with both feet. God knew Joseph's commitment would keep him in God's will.

Without a solid commitment in a relationship, the walls around the heart are not protected. Commitment equals protection. When a man and a woman become emotionally and spiritually intimate without commitment, one of two things will happen: they will marry or they will break up. God the protector asks us to "guard our hearts for it is the wellspring of life" (Prov. 4:23 NIV). There is a role here that we must play to avoid being hurt by emotional and spiritual intimacies outside of God's will. God's Word tells us to protect our hearts. Guarding your heart will require you to discern when to share and when to hold back. Pray that God will sensitize you in ways of protecting your heart. Should we play this role to just avoid being hurt? No, we do it because it may harden our hearts toward God and He's protecting us from this occurring.

Broken hearts do not mend easily. With every emotional tie that is damaged by an emotional break up, the heart grows more calloused. Then walls are built up around it for protection. Little pieces of the heart are lost every time people go together and break up. If this happens too often, a heart can shut down and become bitter. Also, if the heart is too callous, it will be difficult for a future spouse to soften. Our goal is to give our mates soft hearts that become emotionally intimate quickly.

This task is not an easy one, but it is essential if the goal—to save all of one's heart for one's future mate—is to be fulfilled. For some, protecting their hearts may require less flirting; for others it may require not giving special attention to a friend.

Let's apply the commitment-then-intimacy idea to same-sex friendships, siblings, parents or teachers. How many of us desire to be intimate with others who are not proven trustworthy or loyal or who have ulterior motive? How many of us have commitment-free friendships? Do we trust those who have not proven to be dependable? Of course, heartache can occur in a same-sex friendship, but not because one is left disappointed the relationship was not moving towards a romantic level. The expectation of a future with same-sex friendships is quite different.

I have a dear friend who received e-mail from a guy friend. He said she was beautiful, and told her how her new haircut added to her beauty. He went on to say he'd like to write to her, and nonchalantly added that he was "single again." What would you make of this letter? My friend knew this guy was not God's choice for her, so she let him know that what he said was way out of the bounds of their friendship. She informed him that their relationship would never lead to matrimony. He responded with an angry e-mail, accusing her of being the one who was out of line because he never mentioned matrimony.

What was he doing? He was asking, in a back-door manner, for her heart with no commitment. When she confronted him, he characteristically shifted blame to the woman. This story was reminiscent of the Adam and Eve syndrome: "The women you gave to me made me do it." (Genesis 3:12)

If Christian singles made a pledge to not pursue an intimate relationship with another person without the explicit intent of taking the relationship to marriage, I believe, there would be more people married and fewer divorced in the Christian culture.

The *need* for a marriage partner is non-existent, absent, missing and gone when emotions are *freely* bestowed on anyone who comes along. My sisters and I hope our husbands are starving for female attention. See, if my partner is lonely for female attention and companionship he will appreciate me a great deal more than if other girl friends had filled in my place before God introduces us.

God is the God of this protected covenant. The commitment you make to God when you choose to accept the gift of salvation allows complete, open and honest communion with God. When someone has had a string of friends or boy/girlfriends who let them down, how will that person fully trust that it won't happen again? God can heal many hurt hearts. Learn to trust God with your emotions. He longs to protect you with His healthy boundaries. Let's look at how God expresses His open door of intimacy after we commit ourselves to Him.

Shouldn't friendship be the basis of a relationship, especially marriage? How do you know if you could marry someone if you do not become intimate friends first? Are you allowed to be intimate with God before commitment? Is your relationship with God based on friendship? Since the church is the bride of Christ, are we friends first and then a bride? No! After you commit your whole life to Him, the doors to the holy of holies open.

When God gave Moses the blueprint for the tabernacle He created a room where the priests would meet Him, the holy of holies. A veil, approximately four inches thick, separated the room from the rest of the tabernacle. Priests were allowed into this sanctuary (Heb. 9:7); the blood of their animal sacrifices allowed them to enter. This was a place of supreme intimacy with the Father, where only a priest could meet with Him on behalf of others (Exod. 25:22). We see now all are invited into this place through Christ's death.

> Therefore, brethren, since we have this confidence to enter the holy place by the blood of Jesus, by a new and living way which He inaugurated for us through the veil, that is, His flesh (Heb.10:19-20).

The author of Hebrews is talking to the brethren. He spoke to his brothers and sisters in the Lord. To enter into that family one must accept Jesus as personal Lord and Savior. We are adopted into God's family (Gal. 4:5). Only *after* we enter into a life-long commitment with God may we come into the holy of holies. Step one: a life-long commitment. Step two: you have intimacy with Him. It is impossible to love Him before step one and He does not let us "get to know Him" personally before the commitment.

God created marriage to be an example of the relationship between Christ, the bridegroom, and the church, His bride (Eph. 5:23,24; Rev. 19:7-9; 21:2). Why should our path toward earthly marriage look or act differently? Our path should be commitment and then intimacy.

The no-intimate-relationship-without-a-commitment lifestyle may not be the easiest road to travel. God's ways are difficult and at times it may feel as though we are swimming upstream. His ways always have long-term benefits; unfortunately, we have a tendency to gravitate to the short-term pleasures of the moment. God desires us to be obedient, and then the blessings follow. Obedience to Him expresses our love for Him. We see in Philippians 2:8-11 that,

> Christ humbled Himself by becoming obedient to the point of death, even death on a cross. Therefore also,

God highly exalted Him and bestowed on Him the name
which is above every name so that every knee will bow
and every tongue will confess that Jesus Christ is Lord.

We need to be alert to emotional and spiritual purity
with others and choose wisely those with whom we share
our hearts, emotions, and minds. Our hearts are to be
guarded at all costs. God will bless those who seek Him
with a pure heart. He wants us to love Him with our heart,
soul, mind, and strength.

Thought Questions:
1. How would commitment then intimacy aid in
remaining emotional pure?
2. What would you say is your emotional holy of
holies?
3. What are some benefits of having commitment
before intimacy?

The Envy Monster

Have you ever been envious? Envious of someone's job, house, money, marriage? Well, I have. It seems to be a major problem. Many of us have this idea that we deserve to have something, and when we don't get it we pout. This is envy, it's being covetous, it's sin, and it's ugly. But what do we do to rid ourselves of this?

When we allow envy to creep into our lives we allow the envy monster, Satan, to have his way. One pitfall we singles must avoid is having envy toward those who are married.

When I struggled with being single I heard a preacher say, "To be envious is to doubt God's love for you and His sovereignty in your life." Wow! That hit home for me. I did not trust His love for me. I believed the lie that married people were more special to God than me, a single. Just because you are single does not mean God loves you any less than He loves your married friends. God loves you the same. This is a common lie Satan loves to throw our way to take our focus and trust off the Father.

Throughout the Bible envy and covetousness are on the lists of behaviors of the ungodly and those who will not inherit the kingdom.

> For this you know with certainty, that no immoral or impure person or *covetous* man, who is an idolater, has an inheritance in the kingdom of Christ and God (Eph. 5:5 emphasis added).

God desires us to be content with the path He has marked out for us.

A key to having a deep personal relationship with God is contentment. Why? Easy. When you are fully content, you say that you are 100 percent, totally willing to accept whatever God wants to throw your way—the good, the bad, and the ugly. Look at Jesus' heart of contentment toward the Father:

> Have this attitude in yourself, which was also in Christ Jesus, who, although He existed in the form of God, did not regard equality with God a thing to be grasped, but emptied Himself, taking the form of a bond-servant, and being made in the likeness of men. Being found in appearance as a man, He humbled Himself and becoming obedient to the point of death, even death on a cross (Phil. 2:5-8).

Once you fully empty yourself of self, you take on the attitude of Christ Jesus. He may have wanted the "cup" of suffering to be taken from Him (Matt. 26:39), but He went all the way to death to prove His trust in the Father's plans.

Many of us are familiar with Philippians 4:11, in which Paul tells us how he has "learned to be content in whatever circumstance." Notice the word "learned." He did not just—

poof—understand contentment. He learned contentment in God's private classroom of life. When Paul released what he wanted and was shipwrecked, beaten, and jailed all for the sake of Christ, contentment found him. He learned to release his will, to die to his desires and live for Christ. "For me to live is Christ, and to die is gain" (Phil. 1:21). Paul knew death to self was truly living for Christ.

We cannot have godliness without contentment. "But godliness actually is a means of great gain *when accompanied* by contentment" (1 Tim. 6:6 emphasis added). The rich man in Luke 12 was not content with what he had. He planned to build more barns and have good years ahead of him. That very night God required his soul. How much could he have done for the Lord had he found contentment with what he had? Unfortunately, we will never know. What a regretful statement. Often many of us are not content with our lot. When we have discontentment we may be unable to see what God would want for us. This self focus can ruin our walk with Jesus.

Who are we to think we deserve marriage anyway? Actually, we don't deserve anything. God sent His Son to die on the cross so that we have hope of eternal life. We must find contentment in that. Yes, all we need or want should be wrapped up in the fact the Heavenly Father provided a way to have eternal life with Him. We must repent of thinking that this season of our life is too hard, or that anything in life is too difficult. God will not give you more than you can handle (1 Cor. 10:13, Phil. 4:13). God calls us to lay aside foolish and selfish thoughts, to press on, to gird up our loins, push through and fight the good fight. God desires you to find contentment in Him alone. Once you come to a place where you lay aside your expectations of God, then contentment will find you.

When one does not rid their heart of discontentment before marriage, discontentment will creep up within marriage. When one looks to anything but God to bring happiness, He will never allow that other thing to bring satisfaction. One key piece of advice often given to people is make sure you marry someone who is content with the Lord alone. Someone who enters into a marriage without being content with God alone may have a tendency to look to his or her mate as a "savior." That pressure on the "savior" could become overwhelming.

I knew a couple who found the idea of marriage so alluring that they rushed into it. The godly advice they received before marriage was to wait and slow down. Once married, they looked to each other for deep satisfaction. They used each other as idols. A few years later they divorced.

If you want to find someone who is content, you must also have contentment with Christ during your years as a single. But don't try to reach contentment to fool God so He will give you a mate. You'll end up fooling yourself! On the other hand, once you've reached contentment God will not automatically say, "Okay, you're finally content, now I will give you a mate."

Being content with your singleness does not necessarily mean that God has blessed you with the gift of singleness either. Do not let contentment scare you. Making peace with singleness does not equal a life with no possibility for marriage. Once you achieve true contentment with our Lord and Savior, peace will follow.

It boils down to fear. Do you fear being single the rest of your life? Or do you fear being in a marriage not ordained by God? If the fear of being single is greater than the fear of being in the wrong marriage, problems will occur. My mom, sisters, and I call these hysterical fears.

In 1 Peter 3:1-7, Peter addresses wives. He shares what we should strive for: chaste and respectful behavior (vs. 2), external beauty that reflects the internal beauty of a quiet and gentle spirit (vs. 3-4), and adornment through submission to God. In verse 6 it states we will become Sarah's (Abraham's wife) children, "if you do what is right without being frightened by *fear*" (emphasis added). We will achieve these godly qualities, if we are not overcome by our hysterical fears.

Norm Wakefield stated in his book, *Equipped to Love*, "Whenever someone looks to anything or anyone rather than God as the source of all things, he commits the sin of idolatry. This may sound strange, but it's true. Here is a good definition of idolatry: looking to any person, object or idea to supply what only God can supply." We must examine things in our lives that may be idols. Could it be the idea of marriage? Or could it be the "friend" you have?

Recently, on Christian talk radio, a counselor was helping people with their marital problems. This woman caller was desperate for answers and a quick fix for her persistent problem. She'd been married for ten years. She had befriended a Christian man on the Internet. Since she was not receiving emotional support from her husband she turned to her computer friend. The emotions she needed from him prompted him to want a break in their relationship. This thought petrified her. She said, "I feel compelled to talk to him. I can't stop." She was looking for a "savior" of her emotions, someone to fill in the gaps that only God could. This man had become an idol in her life. Remember the term for an idol, "anything you look to for something that only God can give you." She did not go into depth on

Emotional Purity

the history of her marriage, but I can almost guarantee that during the start of her marriage she relied on her husband for the same things she wanted from this Internet friend. She needed to go to her heavenly Father for her emotional support and be content with Him.

Now, how does this relate to us? When discontentment is felt in life, when one does not find true contentment with God alone, problems can easily occur. Ask God to point out areas in your life where you are not content, then ask Him to help you be satisfied with His plan. He will begin to reveal areas where you are not fully in His will. Once this lesson is learned, you may need to lean on God "the Educator" to continue to keep you reminded of His instructions.

If you are married, where do you find your satisfaction? Are you longing for your spouse to fill your empty heart? It will never happen. Only God can fill this hole in your heart. He designed it that way. Your husband has not been created to make you happy. Your wife has not been created to satisfy you always. Look to God to fill this area of your life. Trust Him to take care of your marriage. Be content with where you are in life. As difficult as marriage can be, continue to draw near to God. God can use another person, your mate perhaps, to contribute to your happiness and satisfaction, but remember it ultimately comes from God and He deserves the glory.

In an e-mail my newly married friend Michelle explained this point quite well. "I have learned that marriage does not quell my desires for stability or joy. But that is not a dig on marriage, or mine in particular, it is just to say that the Lord is supreme and His ways are to be desired above all. Because, let me tell you, with the Holy Spirit in you, you will *not* be satisfied even in a great marriage unless you are growing in your relationship with Jesus. He will not let you be happy with things of this earth. Now that I've led you to believe that my marriage is not satisfying all my desires . . . it is truly the most amazing blessing straight from heaven ('cause I could never do anything so perfect). He is so pure and unblemished and genuine and desiring to please me."

Michelle definitely understands that marriage is not the answer to unending joy, but is truly a blessing from God. She found contentment with Christ alone before marriage, and sees her relationship with Him as crucial after marriage. She knows His plan is best.

We have a tendency to not trust in God's plan, and that can cause envy or discontentment. However, let us look at some verses about God's ways compared to our ways.

For my thoughts are not your thoughts, neither are your ways My ways," declares the Lord. "For as the heavens are higher than the earth, so are My ways higher than your ways and My thoughts than your thoughts (Isa. 55:8-9).

Just as you do not know the path of wind and how bones are formed in the womb of the pregnant woman, so you do not know the activity of God who makes all things (Eccles. 11:5).

The plans of the heart belong to man, but the answer of the tongue is from the Lord (Prov. 16:1).

For I know the plans I have for you, declares the Lord. (Jer. 29:11a).

There are many more verses that speak about how God will direct us. We must trust Him. At first we may not understand what God is doing. As David said in Psalms 139:6, "Such knowledge is too wonderful for me; it is too high I cannot attain to it." He was comfortable knowing that he did not know.

There may come a time when we will look back on our single years and see God's fingerprints everywhere. If you have ever read *The Hiding Place* or any other book about godly, single Christians, you will clearly see that God wants us to use our whole lives to give Him glory. The pain, trials, and struggles become clear when you set envy aside. You will see how the ups and downs of life are to be dealt with head on, free from envy.

You've heard "hindsight is 20-20." I think the children of Israel must have coined that phrase. Did they understand what God was going to do when they stood at the Red Sea with their enemies behind them? No. Did they understand or know where their food, water, and provision for their basic needs would come from? No. Did they understand what God did when He said the land He gave to them was filled with giants? No. They continued in their discontentment and the cost became deadly.

The Israelites rebelled against God over and over in the desert, and often we do the same thing. The correlation between the children of Israel and us is clear: they were in bondage to the Egyptians, we are in bondage to believing that marriage is going to save us from this state of discontented singleness. God performed a grand exodus to save the Israelites from slavery; God sent His Son to save us from slavery. He led the Israelites through the desert of testing to worship and serve Him there; He wants us to come through the desert of testing to see if we trust Him. Then He allowed the Israelites to enter the promised land; and, if you allow God to take you through the arid desert of trials, you will come through trusting and obeying Him. The promised land is not marriage, but rather a place of knowing that you are in the Father's hands and that you will not be single a day longer than He plans for you.

Recently I took inventory of how many single friends I have. There are not many left. Many have married and begun to have children. Many of these girlfriends and I would sit around and talk about marriage and worry about when or if we were going to get married. We stirred the cauldron of hysterical fears all the way to the boiling point. Now many of them are married; what a waste of mental energy we spent on worry!

When a thought of discontentment, envy, or lack of trust comes into your head, pray, "Take captive every thought to the obedience of Jesus Christ" (2 Cor, 10:5b). Let the Holy Spirit be your teacher (John 14:26). Let Him provide the learning environment. The pain from this hot desert is His hand conforming you to His likeness.

Also, read verses of God's goodness and His promises for your life. Let these awesome promises from the Father comfort you:

"Bring the whole tithe [What would be your tithe? Waiting patiently for God's time.] into My storehouse . . ." says the Lord, "see if I will not open for you the windows of heaven and pour out for you a blessing until it overflows" (Mal. 3:10).

And the peace of God, which surpasses all comprehension, will guard your hearts and your minds in Christ Jesus (Phil. 4:7).

And the Lord will continually guide you, and satisfy your desire in scorched places, and give strength to your bones; and you will be like a watered garden (Isa. 58:11).

And my God will supply all your needs according to His riches in glory in Christ Jesus (Phil. 4:19).

The Lord will give strength to His people; the Lord will bless His people with peace (Ps. 29:11).

Yet those who wait for the Lord will gain new strength; they will mount up with wings like eagles, they will run and not get tired, they will walk and not become weary (Isa. 40:31).

Can you understand that being envious and not trusting Him can create a wall between you and the Father?

Does it excite you to be at a place of peace about your singleness? Our God is very giving, and we have no business seeking to please our wills (flesh). Only He can satisfy the deepest longings of our souls. Throw off your envy and discontentment, fall on your knees, and trust in an all-loving, all-powerful, completely organized and faithful God.

Thought Questions:
1. When in your life has the sin of envy become all consuming?
2. According to Norm Wakefield's definition of idolatry, on page 89, what are things in your life that would be classified as an idol?
3. What's stopping you from fully trusting God to provide for all your needs?

9

The Prize of Life

Do you know anyone who thinks marriage is the best prize in life? Maybe you feel marriage would elevate you to a newer, higher level. Have these thoughts crept into your mind: "If only I were married, then I would be happy. Ah, to have my own family and children to take care of and a husband/wife to share my life with."

An underlying, unspoken feeling in Christian circles seems to be that marriage brings you to a deeper level of spirituality. It is almost as though marriage is the pinnacle of the Christian life.

In *Common Mistakes Singles Make* Mary Whelchel backs up this train of thought.

> There is a very common tendency to think that life hasn't really begun for us yet. We're just making time, flying around in a holding pattern, waiting for this pre-requisite – marriage – before life can truly start. Even though many singles protest that they aren't doing this, they are.

As Christians, we have this ideal of a Christian marriage: husbands loving their wives as Christ loves the church, and wives being submissive to their husbands. We see marriage as a means to unending companionship and deep intimacy. Marriage is a place for companionship and intimacy, but when we experiment with satisfying those desires on our own, we will be let down. Tracy found in Luke a deep friendship and he made her feel a certain way. However, when Tracy finally says, "I do," will her husband satisfy her emotional needs the same as Luke? What if he cannot satisfy them as well as Luke? What if she never feels as connected emotionally with her husband as she did with Luke? She will continually compare the two and this comparison can lead to discontentment in her marriage.

If I were to compare all my married friends, I would have to say overall my non-Christian friends are more content in their marriages than my Christian friends. As I mentioned earlier, a person who enters into marriage not fully content in the Lord may look to his or her spouse to provide contentment. But remember, God does not allow anything except Himself to make us fully content. So my non-Christian friends marry with a much lower expectation as to how their mate will satisfy their needs. In a recent conversation with a married, Christian girlfriend about this issue, she said her expectations were high going into her marriage. When her mate did not prove to be the exact copy of what the Bible says about a husband, she had to look to God to find peace.

Among my happily married Christian friends, I see a common thread. First, they each went into marriage with an attitude to give 110 percent, not with a what-can-I-gain-from-this attitude. Second, their hearts were thankful to have someone with whom to worship and serve God. Third, they had realistic expectations. They did not depend on their mates to be a vending machine of emotions and actions they could throw their change into and have personal desires met. Commitment, communication and Christ made up their formula to make their marriage God honoring.

What makes this prize-of-life-attitude worse is that older Christian's feed into this lie. They seem to pity the single and revere the married. My sister went through a Bible study workbook with our aunt, who is not much older than we are. The study was titled *Homemaking*. Since our aunt is married she asked if they could study some issues that may be helpful for her. When they opened the book, they read this sentence from the chapter called "Your Divine Task": "Marriage ushers in a safe haven after the loneliness and problems of single life." What kind of statement is that?

A "safe haven" with no more loneliness! I have married friends who would say this statement does not describe their marriages. Yes, marriage should provide a safe haven and your mate does provide companionship, but there are times in a marriage one may experience both insecurity and loneliness. Marriage in and of itself will not bring about satisfaction or solutions to your problems. God is the One who provides that.

Another factor that contributes to this attitude, of elevating marriage to an idol status, is physical intimacy. Most Christians desire to be virgins on their wedding day. (It breaks my heart that I have not known many to fulfill this part of God's plan in this aspect of becoming man and wife before marriage. May God's Word pierce our hearts and drive us to remain pure.) When a couple becomes involved physically, yet they want to wait until their wedding night, they place a great deal of emphasis on the act itself. Each time they have to restrain themselves and not complete the act that God created, they continue to build this idea that marriage will allow the freedom to go "all the way."

Most married couples say that physical intimacy is a small part of marriage, yet for some reason, the permission

to have sex after wedding vows have been spoken is con-
veyed in our Christian culture to be one of the most important aspects of marriage. I have heard a few engaged
Christian men say, "Only X amount of days until it is
legal!" or "After we are married I can have it as much as I
want." When engaged couples fully experience emotional
and spiritual intimacy before marriage, what is there to look
forward to on their wedding day?

There is physical freedom in marriage. Yet too often that
is the only special territory left to await marriage. When we
are already emotionally and spiritually intimate, the only
act to complete the marriage union is sexual intercourse.
This is not how God wants it to be. If we vow to remain
pure physically, emotionally, and spiritually before marriage,
this will leave much uncharted territory to discover after
marriage. Physical intimacy will not be the only undiscov-
ered area. Wouldn't it be exciting to know that you and
your spouse will have many new discoveries to make together? And that your spouse hasn't had the same discoveries with an ex boy/girlfriend or even a "good friend"? It is
exciting to me! That is true romance.

This may scare the living day lights out of some of you
because it raises many questions: "What if we never connect on that deep level after marriage? What if our feelings
never measure up to what I think they should? What if I
never have those feelings for love that you suggest I save?
What if we are not physically compatible? What if . . . ?"
Ask yourself this question: Is God cruel? In your prayer
life, if you are asking for a kind, gentle, considerate mate
do you think God will give you a mean, insensitive, rude
mate? God is not out there planning how to make you miserable. When you obey Him, He blesses you. We do not
serve a malicious God who will pull a fast one on us.

Ask, and it will be given to you . . . what man is there among you who, when his son asks for a loaf will give him a stone . . . If you then, being evil, know how to give good gifts to your children, how much more will your Father who is in heaven give what is good to those who ask Him (Matt. 7:7-11).

Let that encourage you.

Next to salvation, your choice of mate is the biggest decision of your life. God is not going to leave you hanging. Marriage is created to paint a picture of our relationship with Him. He desires your marriage to bring Him glory. Satan, on the other hand, loves to rob you of your faith and trust. Satan plays mind games and wants you to think you need to do things the way the world does things in order to find happiness. No, we find our joy in things not of this world.

How much did you know about the Christian walk and faith when you began your life-long commitment to God? You didn't know much; you relied on your faith. Why do you feel you need to know it *all* before a commitment in a relationship? Where is your faith on this issue? It may take gut-wrenching faith to save your emotions for your mate; it also takes gut-wrenching faith to commit yourself to God. Is your testimony like the guy's next to you? No, coming into a relationship with God is different for each of us, but the conclusion is the same. Likewise with marriage; all of our paths to meeting our spouses may look different, but in the end we are married.

The prize of life is a relationship with our Creator. To look to anything else to fill that gap will not bring about satisfaction. God designed marriage but He designed us to be complete when we are with Him. Marriage is not the answer to eternal bliss. To give it that much credit is taking away credit from the Creator. Marriage is a blessing, not *the blessing*! A deeper walk with the Lord is not to be brought about by marriage, alone, but by reading His Word, talking to Him, obeying Him and giving Him praise, glory and honor.

Thought Questions:
1. How has the marriage-is-the-prize-of-life attitude effected you?
2. What "uncharted territory" do you want to have with your mate?
3. In your own words, describe your prize of life.

10

Become Friends with Your Feelings

eelings. It seems as if everyone is talking about feelings. Randomly surfing either radio or TV, you're sure to hear this topic discussed. Counselors' schedules are packed with despondent people searching for a remedy to the emptiness they feel. One well-known counselor's web page claimed to "see over 3000 patients each week." In school it seems more important how students feel about themselves than how much they learn. "I feel . . ." or "How does that make you feel?" became an identifying catch phrases of the 1990s, for sure!

We have become a culture absorbed with feelings. It's what we do with our feelings and whom we turn to for relief that makes the difference. God has feelings such as jealousy, grief, joy, sorrow, friendship, etc. God, the Creator of all, even created emotions.

Feelings have become great foundations for stories and characters. On *Star Trek: The Next Generation* Data, an android, looks, talks, walks, and acts like a human. The one difference in this character is a void of feelings. In one episode they implanted in him a computer chip of emotions and feelings, with interesting results. A character in the original *Star Trek* is Spock, half human, half Vulcan. As a Vulcan he prides himself on being able to suppress his feelings. Episodes have shown what happens when he lets his emotions go, again very interesting. The subplot of my story of Tracy and Luke is what she felt about Luke. Feelings are a large part of our lives but, as some will say, can you trust them?

As singles we seem to have feelings running wild through our veins. We pulse with loneliness, frustration, envy, confusion and a host of other uncomfortable feelings. Being single can bring on a set of emotions that dash ahead of our rational thoughts. God gave us the ability to feel and love, but when we focus on how we feel it may cause us to lose sight of why God gave this human capacity.

Let's look at the two types of feelings we have the ability to experience.

First we have foundational feelings. These feelings are answers to our deep questions such as: What is the meaning of life? and What is my purpose? A believer should have a fundamental sense of who they are according to God. The goal of a believer is "to love the Lord your God with all your heart and with all your soul and with all your mind" (Matt. 22:37). A person who does not know God, or is not known by God, holds no answers to those questions. God set eternity in the hearts of all men (Eccles. 3:11), and once we know we have eternal life this void is satisfied in our hearts. Many have heard that we have a God-shaped vacuum in our heart; when we come to know Him this empty vacuum is filled. Our identity in Christ provides us peaceful feelings deep in our hearts. These resulting deep foundational feelings of hope of eternal life (Titus 1:2; 3:7) should not waver according our situation, thoughts, attitudes, or moods.

God's written will for our life can be compared to these foundational feelings. We read His will for us in His Word, such as, "Do not lay up for yourselves treasures upon earth" (Matt. 6:19a) or "Do not be worried about your life" (Matt. 6:25a). This written will from God for our lives is unchanging and will not waver based on situations, thoughts, attitudes, or moods. So these foundational feelings of who we are—"a chosen race, a royal priesthood, a holy nation, a people for God's own possession" (1 Pet. 2:9)—should not waver. God's Word provides a constant, stable base of peace at the core of our souls.

The second type of feeling we experience are surface feelings. These change daily and are a reaction to what may be going on in our hearts. For example, we find out a friend is having a baby and we feel joy and excitement. We step onto a roller coaster and we feel scared and anxious. We start a new job and we feel awkward and clumsy. We see a wedding on TV and we feel envious and frustrated. In life, things come our way and these surface feelings change depending on the situations. Have you ever seen a movie that takes you from crying to laughing, from frustration to peace? To run the gamut of all emotions is not uncommon in a movie, and it can leave us drained of any feelings.

Just as our foundational feelings reflect God's written will, our surface feelings may be compared to God's plan for our lives. God's plan for individual lives is not written in black and white. Each day we seek to find what He would want us to do and obey it step by step. For example, you may be considering a job transfer. God's written word says to work hard (Col. 3:23) and not to be in debt to anyone (Rom. 13:8) among other things. If this job transfer lines up with God's written Word, then you must seek Him through prayer, godly wisdom, the prompting of the Holy Spirit, and by using the mind He gave you to make the choice. Just as God's plan for our lives may shift, it should never contradict His written will; our surface feelings will change, but they should not disagree with our foundational sense of who we are in the Lord.

Christian singles, both men and women, have this look of "Hey, I'm single; I don't like it, and I won't be happy until I'm married!" Rarely will they verbalize this to anyone but their actions speak volumes. These feelings manifest themselves in different ways. It could be a roll of the eyes at a loving couple or it may be restrained, such as a root of bitterness lurking in the heart.

While I searched for a job a close friend of mine was hired as a flight attendant. I was jealous, mainly because she knew where God wanted her to work. My heart said, *You are employed and I don't like that God is keeping me in the dark right now with the direction of my life.* Of course, when she would talk with excitement about her future I would fake my happiness for her. Then the Holy Spirit convicted me with the verse "Rejoice with those who rejoice" (Rom. 12:15a). I immediately went to my friend and asked her to forgive me. The mask I wore was a massive façade, hiding a covetous heart full of envy.

This wasn't about being jealous of someone's marital status but of some*thing* someone had that I wanted. If we put on a show of happiness, excitement, or joy when our feelings are the complete opposite, we are lying. Not a good thing. Being honest with my friend led to a life lesson, which helped me to understand that I must be content where God had me at the moment. I have no right to think He loves my other brothers and sisters in Christ more just because they have a job, a mate, or anything else I think I deserve.

Another way feelings act out is when a person makes it clear that they are available, and may even come across to others as different than who they really are in order to appear as "marriage material." How might one appear different? Perhaps by laughing a little louder at a "prospect's" joke, agreeing with ideas or actions you're not totally comfortable with, or sharing how God is teaching and growing you with the hope of attracting a mate with the boasting of your godly character and qualities. In general, by acting and manipulating. Putting on a show. I have seen it. I have done it. We can all be good actors when there is someone to impress.

I'll make a confession here to help you fully understand what I am saying. One night I attended a picnic that a male "single prospect" also attended. I wanted him to see my heart of serving so I jumped up as soon as I finished eating, picked up plates, did dishes, stacked chairs, and emptied trash. Why did I do this? In the hope this man would see me as the good servant of the Lord that I was. Again, Heather learns another life lesson. Not only did he not notice me, but no one noticed I was such a good helper! This was what I call a "Hello, Heather!" moment. The Holy Spirit said, "Hello, Heather, when you are serving to please man, how can you please God?" (Gal. 1:10) Until my motives were pure, I did not lift a finger in front of anyone. Now, I am sure some thought I was lazy, but God molded me into the servant *He* wanted me to be.

This is the category Tracy found herself in. Tracy did not tell anyone she thought she would be married by now. She "opened up" to Luke beyond her comfort level in hopes of being more attractive to him; therefore putting her timing above God's timing.

When we are caught up in a friendship, as Tracy and Luke were, unpleasant feelings of wanting marriage may subside due to the hope of this friendship possibly materializing into a permanent relationship. Tracy may have found contentment with where God had her at the moment because she tasted what she wanted, but those ugly feelings would only return when their friendship ended.

We all know single people who make their sad case of singleness to all their friends. They make sure everyone knows they are on the hunt for that special someone. They scan the personals section hoping to find "the one." Or they register with Christian on-line dating services that encourage participants to post their picture and a short bio to attract Mr. or Miss Right. These unmarried people seem to flaunt their empty ring finger and mention to everyone their intense desire to be married. The desire to be married is not wrong, but how you react to the desire can overshadow your service to the Lord.

In the situations mentioned above, one's feelings about not being married can change based on how others respond to one's complaints on "single life insecurities." Well-meaning friends will say things to heal a lonely heart, such as, "You will make a great wife/husband!" "Keep looking— they have to be out there somewhere." People will feed into this idea that marriage will quench emptiness, when in reality only looking to the Source will satisfy. When one looks to others as a means to satisfy emotions, one is making that person an idol and God will never let an idol be satisfying.

Many people involved in groups of singles will feed into each other. They can become so wrapped up in their singleness that the topic is all they study or talk about. Yes, talking about and understanding the journey through the single years should help us focus more on serving the Lord, but obsessing about it will only lead to further discontentment.

I have seen friends who busy themselves to avoid feelings of loneliness and dissatisfaction. Running to work, to Bible study, to the gym, to lunch, to a weekend here, to a weekend there, to the movies, to the bowling alley, to church, to choir, to get coffee, to praise band practice, to the post office, to the laundromat, to the grocery store, to the bank, to the car wash . . . And the list goes on. Do you feel as though you are in a whirlwind?

Most of these activities are important, but should be kept in their proper place. The things we do should not be used as a method to avoid obeying what God wants for us. Nor should we bury unwanted feelings in schedules full of hectic activity.

I'll add to the list of deterrents: sleeping too much, overeating, under-eating, excessive spending, smoking, over-exercise, gossiping, disproportionate working, gambling, drunkenness, pornography, anti-depressants, unhealthy relationships, obsessive self-focus, sports, and a host of other things can become deterrents to what we feel. Some people turn to alcohol to drift off to dreamland and forget reality, but we could use any of the above-mentioned activities to do the same thing. We are flesh and in our flesh we have a tendency to look for worldly things and activities to keep us happy.

"Search me, O God, and know my heart; try me and know my anxious thoughts; and see if there be any hurtful way in me, and lead me in the everlasting way" (Ps. 139:23-24).

When one keeps busy to avoid something, one may not have time to be still before God. He asks us to be still before Him. "Cease striving and know that I am God" (Ps. 46:10a). One reason for this is to quiet our hearts and let Him examine our deepest layers.

Quieting our hearts and being still before God will allow Him to move and fight for us in situations. Exodus 14:14 states, "The Lord will fight for you; you need only to be still."

God wants to be the God of your feelings. Your only task is to let Him be God. When we step ahead we get in His way. God gives deliverance from ungodly emptiness or lonely feelings. He can do anything He wants. We have to move out of the way.

Let's take the example of my friend, who was gainfully employed, and me waiting on God's direction. The Holy Spirit sometimes speaks in a whisper, so when our lives and minds are busy it can be hard to hear. Let's say I faked being happy for her and kept myself busy with activities to put an end to this unlikable feeling. I may have searched harder for a job and resented her without being able to fully understand why. This resentment could have grown until I truly disliked her. I could have become bitter toward God and then one day wondered why I felt that way. Thankfully, my heart found peace and heard the Holy Spirit teach me the lesson He meant for me to learn.

Finding satisfaction is a beautiful thing. The root reasons for feeling incomplete or unsatisfied are: one, we are not relying on the foundational feelings of who we are in Christ, and two, we are being discontent with where God has us.

I spent a year working in a ministry in Denver, Colorado. This ministry required a great deal of laying aside my own wants and wishes. Without a shadow of a doubt I knew God wanted me there. Being content with that knowledge allowed me to face each trial with a deep understanding of my purpose. Had I been discontented I might have not learned the lessons God taught me that year.

An example of this came one snowy evening when one of the at-risk teens ran away from the facility. We were up almost all night with a search team out looking and another group keeping the other teens under control back at the house. I could have been upset by this whole situation, but my confidence rested in the fact God wanted me there.

Why do we rely on our surface feelings to dictate happiness or sadness, satisfaction, or disappointment? It may be caused by our tendency to forget our true identity. Take a few moments and read out loud the list below of what God thinks of you.

I am a person for God's own possession (1 Pet. 2:9).

I am God's child and I call Him Abba Father (Rom. 8:15).

I am redeemed through Him and have forgiveness (Eph. 1:7).

God loves me and I am precious in His sight (Isa. 43:4).

I am lifted and carried by God through all trials (Isa. 63:9).

I am to receive God's blessing when I obey Him (Rom. 8:28).

Surface feelings can be changed, heightened, or numbed by our surroundings and by the things we watch, read, or talk about. When we rely on our feelings of dissatisfaction to determine how we will act or think, we toss God's Word and His power aside.

The list above is in no way a complete catalog all of the references of God's feelings toward you. As you continue to study the Word, ask God to reveal all that's mentioned of His loving, tender feelings toward you, and then rely on *those feelings*. Know that God is the One who satisfies and makes us complete.

Finally, spend time before Him and quiet your heart. Allow God to show you how He feels about you. Seek Him first—not a mate. Give Him your heart and His blessings will follow your obedience.

Learning to manage your unruly feelings may be difficult at first, but as you realize that God is the God of all feelings it will become easier. He wants us to place all our hopes and feelings into the palm of His hand and leave them there for His use. As you strive toward a deeper level of trust with your emotions, waiting for His timing will be a beautiful season in your spiritual life.

Thought Questions:
1. How do you keep your, sometimes unruly, surface feelings lined up with the core of whom God made you?
2. Can you think of a time in your life when you put on an act to temporarily set aside some unwanted surface feelings? What happened?
3. Go to the list on page 107, have any of those activities been a deterrent in your life?

11

Become Friends with Your Expectations

Have you ever made plans for a day of shopping? You want to go here and then there. Enjoy lunch at this special restaurant and end the day with a show at the local theater. You meet up with your shopping partner, who has a different set of plans. She wants to eat at a fast-food joint, shop at one mall, and definitely does not want to see a movie. What does this do to your expectations? It shoots them down. At that point you have two ways to re-act: selfishly or unselfishly. We can go off into the world of annoyance and disappointment or we can accept what is before us and go on with life.

We expect all kinds of things, from all kinds of people, in all kinds of ways. We expect people waiting on us at the store to be kind and attentive. We expect our food to be served quickly at a restaurant. We expect our boss to give us a big raise. We expect mom to always be there for us. We expect our friends to know better. Life is full of expecta-tions. What we need to know is how we react when our expectations are not met. What makes or breaks us in the situation? And even more, how does our behavior effect another person's expectations?

When we cling to our expectations we are saying we know what should happen or what would be best in a given situation. This nasty "cling" is pride. Any time we believe we hold the keys to what would be best in any circumstance, we become a god. Eve thought she knew what would be best and her expectation was to finally have her eyes opened to the knowledge of God.

When I find myself frustrated, angry, annoyed, or having a stinky attitude, it is because of an unfulfilled expectation. This nips at me all the time. Learning to set aside unmet expectations unselfishly can be difficult.

Have you thought, "I should be married by now!" Or "Why are kids I used to babysit for getting married and not me?" (Two girls I used to babysit have married in the past couple of years.) When you place an expectation on a situation and it is not met, the flesh has a tendency to take over. This expectation attitude allows Satan to get a foothold in our minds and causes us not to trust God.

> For our weapons of warfare are not of the flesh, but divinely powerful for the destruction of fortresses. We are destroying speculations [expectations] and every lofty thing raised up against the knowledge of God, and we are taking every thought captive to the obedience of Jesus Christ (2 Cor. 10:4-5).

This is a powerful verse when it comes to allowing our expectations to not rule over reality or rational thought. If you look up "fortress" in a thesaurus you will find terms such as stronghold, vice-like grip, monopoly, stranglehold, and iron grip. Wow—to know that when we put on our divine armor we can literally throw down Satan, with his schemes that keep us locked up!

Our Lord and Savior broke the chains of the destructive fortresses. Fortresses, such as looking to marriage to "save us," are broken with the power of Jesus. We have to believe and pray that God will allow us to "lay aside every encumbrance and the sin which so easily entangles us; and let us run the race that is set before us, fixing our eyes on Jesus, the author and perfecter of faith" (Heb. 12:1b-2a).

Have you felt at times that things in your life keep you mentally weighed down? Have you felt that spiritual pull on your mind? It becomes frustrating when we are not tapped into the Source, Who can, with a simple blow, destroy those chains that bind.

We must renew our minds daily if we are going to have a renewing of our reactions to unmet expectations. "Therefore if you have been raised up with Christ, keep seeking the things above, where Christ is seated at the right hand of God. Set your mind on things above, not on the things that are on earth" (Col. 3:1-2).

When you commit your life to Christ, you should strive to set your mind on things above. Paul tells us here to "keep seeking," keep moving forward. Ephesians 4:15 states, "we are to grow up in all aspects into Him who is the head." This process of renewing is ongoing and with God's help you will grow closer to Him.

"Hey, I have tried to take captive every thought and set my mind on things above and it just does not work, I still feel cheated by God in the marriage department and He never allows me to have what I want," one may say. When you have a thought not focused on God, not honoring God, or when you expect something that does not come into reality, what do you do? Do you allow it to grow and fester it in your mind? Do you dwell on the unattainable? This is where the battle begins.

Okay, my friend, this may be hard to explain because it deals with the inner thoughts and motives of people. Each one of us has to ask God what honors Him.

> Finally, brethren, whatever is true, whatever is honorable, whatever is right, whatever is pure, whatever is lovely, whatever is of good repute, if there is any excellence and if anything worthy of praise, let your mind dwell on these things (Phil. 4:8).

These are the things God desires us to think upon. Keeping our thoughts pure will help us keep our emotions pure.

When I desired a relationship with a male friend I would go over imaginary conversations in my head. My expectation elevated with each forged tête-à-tête. Was this honoring God? I would say no. Reread Philippians 4:8, "Whatever is true . . ." Were these chats true? No, it was Heather wasting mental energy on relational fantasies.

Tracy's heart could have been spared the pain if she had avoided thinking Luke was going to return her feelings. She allowed herself to read into too many of Luke's actions. Had she taken captive each thought about Luke and their potential future her heart would have been more protected. Our minds have become a battlefield. We need to recognize the battle and declare war.

We need to come up with battle plans. My plan was this: when I found myself drifting to the world of make believe I prayed, "Take captive every thought to the obedience of Christ." This helped a great deal, and before I knew it I was not wasting mental energy on bogus conversations. My sister tells me she prays, "Take captive every thought to the obedience of Christ and soon you'll be thinking of some-thing nice." This rhyme helps her stay focused.

Women, especially, know what I mean when it comes to controlling our emotional thoughts. A well-meaning Christian male befriends you and, before you know it, out of the blue, wedding plans burst into your thoughts and your name, transformed to Mrs. His Last Name, repeats itself in your wandering mind. Can't you just hear Tracy thinking "Mrs. Luke Hartman"?

Raise your hand if you have ever been guilty of this mindless exercise. Oh, I see all hands are raised.

I want to share with you a story about my sister who struggled with this mindless exercise. She had recently joined a singles group and befriended a young man who went on an extended mission trip not long after they met. During the trip he wrote her letters to share with the whole group. One week she received a letter that included one for the group and one for her. On the top of the page he had written, "for you only," in large print.

The letter opened with the common basic pleasantries of asking how she was, and typical small talk. Then, "Hey . . . I just wanted you to know I think that it is neat you are taking such a major step in ministry. I just want you to be encouraged that I am behind you 100 percent. I'll continue to pray for you and look forward to seeing how God uses you. If you ever need anything, know that I am there for you. Maybe we can run a couple of [camping] trips this fall. Love in Christ."

You might think this letter was an innocent letter of encouragement, but my sister struggled with not thinking more of this young man than just a brother in Christ. She expected there to be more of relationship between them but when he came home, God showed her this man was not to be her husband. Her spent emotions and mental energy were wasted.

Mindless exercise can become a vicious cycle. Mental strife can lead to "striving after the wind" (Eccles. 1:14b), which is futile. When a fantasy starts you need to combat it with the Word, and take captive every thought to the obedience of Jesus Christ. I do not mean ungodly fantasies, but the ones about a conversation you would love to have with a special person, the things you could do together, the jokes you could tell, the sunsets you could enjoy together. Even about how great marriage would be, how you would feel in a wedding dress . . . The list goes on. Of course, having hope of all these things is not the problem. The problem is when this hope turns into a mental stronghold or when focus on these hopes outweights the focus on God. Each of these fantasies or expectations can lead us to a dangerous passage of self-focus and self-pity.

How is this a vicious cycle? I grew up near Chicago and many winters of snow have taught me a thing or two. First, never stick your tongue on a metal bar outside. Second, always wear layers. Finally, when you build a snowman make sure the snow is wet.

To wake up and find lots of snow on the ground is one of the greatest things for a child. A day to build snowmen, sled, and drink hot chocolate is a winter wonderland come true. Once mom finished bundling me up in snowsuit and moon boots, out the door I would run. With excitement I would fall on my back and make snow angels. To discover that the snow was light and fluffy was a great disappointment because building a snowman with fluffy snow is close to impossible. The snow has to be a little wet and a bit heavy. Dad didn't like to shovel heavy, wet snow, but we all knew that many snowmen could be built. When the snow was wet and sloppy we would start with a small snowball and create a six-foot-tall round man with stick arms to proudly show off to the neighborhood. It didn't take much effort to put him together when the snow was cooperative.

Just as wet, sticky snow makes small snowballs very quickly into large ones, so does our mind create something from practically nothing. When we are not controlling our mind the results can have a snowball effect, becoming larger with time. Our expectations must be kept in check because it is the "little foxes that are ruining the vineyards" (Song of Sol. 2:15). Unchecked expectations can destroy friendships and break hearts.

In a nutshell, it takes self-control of the mind. When you "walk by the Spirit . . . you will not carry out the desires of the flesh. For the flesh sets its desire against the Spirit and the Spirit against the flesh; for these are in opposition to one another . . . the fruit of the Spirit is . . . self-control" (Gal. 5:16-17; 22-23).

God knew people would indulge their minds. "Among them we too all *formerly lived* in the lusts of our flesh, *indulging* the desires of the flesh and of the *mind*" (Eph. 2:3; emphasis added).

This indulgence needs to be done away with when we become new in Him. Again remember what Paul told the Philippians to think on, "Whatever is true . . . honorable . . . right . . . pure . . . lovely . . . good repute . . . anything excellent and worthy of praise" (Phil. 4:8). Thinking on these things will keep our expectations in check with the Word.

If we do not learn to control our thoughts as a single person, they will be even more difficult to control when we are married. Whether you are a man or a woman your thought life must be under control before marriage or it will haunt you afterward.

Women, if you let yourself become wrapped up in your expectations, and then your husband does not live up to your expectations when you are married these ungodly fantasies may reappear. Maybe this scenario could help.

A married woman feels emotionally distant from her husband. She'd thought that once she was married she'd never be lonely again. She does not know where that closeness went, but she longs to feel emotionally connected to someone. The new pastor starts counseling her to help unravel these feelings. The pastor maintains healthy boundaries, never becoming personal with her. He helps her uncover problems in her marriage. During their sessions the woman starts to notice the small details the pastor remembers and the way he is sensitive to her needs. Before she knows what is happening, her mind cannot stop thinking about the pastor. When he preaches, she thinks of the positive qualities he possesses that her husband lacks. Expectations of her husband become emotional mountains he is unable to scale, and discontentment reeks through every fiber of her being. All because she was unable to keep her thoughts in check.

For men, your thought life may be a little different. You may not ponder what her name sounds like next to your last name, but you may indulge in lustful thoughts that are ungodly. "But I say to you, that every one who looks on a woman to lust for her has committed adultery with her already in his heart" (Matt. 5:28).

Your sex life may look different than you imagined when you are married, and if you are easily attracted to pornography now, it will not end once you are married. Again, if your thought life is not under submission to God then these thoughts will plague you even after you are married.

We must strive toward complete contentment with the life God has given us. Each season of life will present opportunities for growth, and we should long for God to enroll us in His private school. Unmet expectations are a part of life, and knowing how to deal with them in a godly fashion is an excellent skill to learn.

We need to keep our own feelings and expectations in line with what God says. Also, we must not invoke feelings or raise expectations in another person when there is no commitment to take the relationship to another level. We need to be careful how others could perceive our actions.

Let me explain it in this way. Men, when a woman dresses in alluring clothes, what is your reaction? It could be lust, or it could be an attitude of "Please dress modestly so that I will not stumble." We women must realize how visually minded men are, and because of that we should wear modest clothes. It is not because we don't have the right to wear what we want, but it is for the benefit of the spiritual life of our brothers in Christ.

For women, when a guy friend pays special attention to us such as inviting us to his folks' for Sunday dinner, calling just to chat, sharing dreams, sharing struggles, or simply setting us apart from others, what does that do to our hearts? It usually sends us dreaming of the land of marriage and temporarily fills our emotional needs. Men need to realize how emotionally charged women are and avoid causing them to imagine more than what is really there. Men can also be emotionally charged by the actions of a well-meaning friend. We all have to be pure in our actions toward our fellow brothers and sisters in the Lord.

Just recently I explained this concept to a brother in the Lord. He could understand when I said women are as emotionally charged as men are visually charged. He said, "Oh, so a woman can be emotionally married like a man can be visually married in his mind." A beautiful light-bulb moment!

We have to be aware of how others react to our actions. "Therefore let us . . . determine this, not to put an obstacle or stumbling block in a brother's way" (Rom. 14:13). It is acceptable in this society to have a "that's their problem" mindset, but the Word teaches us the complete opposite.

We each have an important role when it comes to how we present ourselves to others. Luke should have been aware his playful nudges, tight hugs, and soft pecks were causing Tracy to feel as though she were someone special to him. His actions suggested there was more to the friendship, but his words, "Oh, no we're just great friends," showed his true feelings.

I have heard that a man can undress a woman in his mind in less than 10 seconds. Well a woman can be emotionally married in her mind in less than 10 seconds. Both men and women need to strive toward purity in all that they do and say toward each other.

Practically, what does this look like? It is pretty simple. Avoid treating friends of the opposite sex special. Treat them as you would anyone else. How did Luke treat Emma? No unusual manner. He never sought her out in a crowd. He didn't call her to just chat. Playful nudges were not part of their friendship and neither were soft pecks good-bye after a holiday weekend with the folks.

Why was it wrong for Tracy and Luke to raise each other's expectations? Did they use each other to gain something they needed—friendship, companionship, workout buddy, emotional connection, or even worse, a feeling of satisfaction? Yes, they defrauded, or took advantage of, one another. We should examine how we act toward those around us and treat them with honesty in ways that will not summon any feeling or expectation that cannot be righteously satisfied by us.

Also, learning how to react to your fellow brothers or sisters in Christ and their unmet expectations and ungodly thoughts with self-control of the mind and actions, will be a testimony of God at work in your life. He longs for us to give our minds to Him. He is the only source of fulfillment, and until we truly understand this we will look for other things to satisfy us. When our minds find freedom from wasted mental energy, then we can abide in the peace and joy of God.

Stop Satan dead in his tracks and fix your mind on Jesus. Have an intense gaze upon Him (Prov. 4:25) and all your ways will be established. Lay your feelings and expectations on His altar and allow Him to be your sole provider, comforter, and companion.

This poem, written by an unknown author, is a beautiful dialog that many of us may have with our Maker when we are feeling frustrated with the quietness of His voice.

WAIT
Desperately, helplessly, longingly, I cried:
Quietly, patiently, lovingly God replied.
I plead and I wept for a clue to my fate,
And the Master so gently said,
"Child, you must wait."

"Wait? You say, wait!" my indignant reply.
"Lord, I need answers, I need to know why!
Is Your hand shortened? Or have You not heard?
By faith, I have asked, and am claiming Your Word.

My future and all to which I can relate
Hangs in the balance, and YOU tell me to WAIT?

I'm needing a "Yes", a go-ahead sign,
Or even a "No" to which I can resign.

And Lord, You promised that if we believe
We need but to ask, and we shall receive.
And Lord, I've been asking, and this is my cry:
"I'm weary of asking! I need a reply!"

Then quietly, softly, I learned of my fate
As my Master replied once again, "You must wait."
So, I slumped in my chair, defeated and taut
And grumbled to God, "So, I'm waiting . . . for what?"

He seemed, then, to kneel
And His eyes wept with mine,
And He tenderly said, "I could give you a sign.
I could shake the heavens, and darken the sun.
I could raise the dead, and cause mountains to run.

All you seek, I could give, and pleased you would be.
You would have what you want~
But, you wouldn't know Me.
You'd not know the depth of My love for each saint;
You'd not know the power I give to the faint;

You'd not learn to see through the clouds of despair;
You'd not learn to trust just by knowing I'm there;
You'd not know the joy of resting in Me;
When darkness and silence were all you could see.

You'd never experience that fullness of love
As the peace of My Spirit descends like a dove;
You'd know that I give and I save, for a start,
But you'd not know the depth of the beat of My heart.

Become Friends with Your Expectations

The glow of My comfort late into the night,
The faith that I give when you walk without sight,
The depth that's beyond getting just what you asked
Of an infinite God, who makes what you have last.

You'd never know, should your pain quickly flee,
What it means that, "My grace is sufficient for thee."
Yes, your dreams for your loved one
Overnight would come true,

But, Oh, the Loss! If I lost what I'm doing in you!

So, be silent, My child, and in time you will see
That the greatest of gifts is to get to know Me.
And though oft' may My answers seem terribly late,
My most precious answer of all is still, "Wait."

Thought Questions:
1. Can you think of a time in your life when an unmet
expectation took over? Explain.
2. What do you do when your thoughts are not God
honoring or self-focused?
3. How can you become friends with your expectations?

12

God's Plan for Your Single Years

ut I want you to be free from concern. One who is unmarried is concerned about the things of the Lord, how he may please the Lord... The woman who is unmarried... is concerned about the things of the Lord that she may be holy both in body and spirit... This I say for your own benefit; not to put a restraint upon you, but to promote what is seemly and to secure undistracted devotion to the Lord (1 Cor. 7:32, 34-35).

"Secure undistracted devotion to the Lord." Briefly consider these few meaty words. Sounds simple, yet living them out in our daily lives may prove to be a stiff assignment. In our society, "keeping ourselves concerned about the things of the Lord" has taken on many definitions, especially when applied to singles.

Why do so many unmarried people have a hard time facing their singleness head on? Mainly because many singles keep themselves wrapped up in activities that do not foster a love relationship with Christ. They do things they want to do (selfishness), without counting the cost that will be paid. They live in the here and now, without a thought of the future. This focus on self permeates this life stage and in many people the years of being single become a wasteland of me, myself, and I, with little concern of serving and enjoying God.

Mary Whelchel puts it plainly in her book *Common Mistakes Singles Make.*

> Let's face it, when you are single . . . it's not difficult to become self-focused. Who else do you really have to consider but yourself? If a single person is not involved in reaching out to other people, that lack of accountability or responsibility to others can produce a selfish life-style.

I realize this may scare some of you, but Jesus was in His thirties and not married. Why does it seem that thirty is such a critical age when it comes to being single? He knew God's will clearly. He was secure in His position with the Father and His purpose was apparent. Therefore, He kept His undivided attention on the Father (Luke 2:49, Matt. 26:39, John 4:34, 17:4).

When singles keep their attention or energy focused on themselves and not on a love relationship with God, they miss out on many activities that would bring about deep satisfaction. Enjoying and serving the Creator should be our number one goal, and this period in our life allows for 100 percent attention on God (". . . but the one that is married is concerned about the things of the world, how he may please his wife...how she may please her husband" 1 Cor. 7 33b, 34b).

We ought to rejoice for this time of undistracted fellowship. This undivided attention to the Lord is the *point* of single life. To use this season in our lives to focus on self does not prepare us for the daily putting aside of self that takes place in marriage. Maybe this is why 50 percent of marriages fail. When one promotes self before marriage, one will still promote self after. When do you think you are going to learn to be unselfish?

In an e-mail conversation a newly married girl friend, Michelle, shared a bit of insight with me, "I will never forget that April [her sister] told me three years ago that if I was preparing myself for marriage – to practice being selfless. Very true – there is simply no room for (selfishness) in a marriage that is to endure years and changes."

Since marriage takes laying aside of our wills and serving another, why not learn this in our single years? If we compare a person who spends their single years focusing on self to a person who is focusing on God, do you think they would look different? You better believe it! Understand that even after marriage all of us will have to continue to die to our wills in some form or another. We should practice becoming unselfish during our single time.

During my teen years I worked at an amusement park. My tasks included operating the rides. This required a time of training and tests before I could take over in the control booth. How did I bless those who rode the ride? Easy—the guest's safety was top priority and I prepared for most emergencies. Now, how many of you would want to ride a roller coaster with an untrained teen at the control booth? I would venture to say none of you. In the same manner that training for roller coaster operation benefited the guest, learning to become a godly, selfless person during your years as a single will bless your mate in ways you cannot imagine. Who would want to marry someone who is unprepared?

What in Tracy and Luke's friendship primed them to shift their focus away from serving and enjoying God? First, they monopolized each other's time. Even if Luke did not reciprocate with special feelings for Tracy, he spent a major portion of time with someone he never thought would be his wife. Think about the time they spent together and let's do some math. Each week has about 48 hours free outside of sleep and work.

Tracy and Luke spent:

Sunday: 3 hours (that is, if it did not extend into the afternoon and evening)

Wednesday: 4 hours

Saturday: another 4 hours at least

That's a total of eleven hours, or 20 percent of their free time, with each other. This time does not include phone calls and e-mail. Wow! What would you do with eleven spare hours each week?

Many singles in our culture have not been told to take advantage of their primary purpose, which God sanctified, for this time in our life. Blessed with this undivided focus, an unmarried person has hours available in a week they could babysit for a young couple at no cost, become a mentor, make an effort to know families in their church, hit their knees in intercessory prayer, develop a deep accountability with an older man or woman . . . And the list could go on. What a waste of time, energy, and mental exercise Luke and Tracy spent on each other and not focusing on God.

"Just as the Son of Man did not come to be served, but to serve, and to give His life . . . So you too, when you do all the things which are commanded you, say, 'We are unworthy slaves; we have done only that which we ought to have done'" (Matt. 20:28 and Luke 17:10). Your purpose in life is clear and simple to understand when you look through spiritual glasses rather than cultural glasses. Christ came to serve and His desire for us is to function likewise during our days as a single.

Instead of focusing on serving God Tracy focused on Luke, their friendship, or a potential future relationship. So, Luke and Tracy's first error was the precious time spent on a futile relationship.

The second error in their relationship was that they appeared to be a couple to those around them. Tracy was "spoken for" in her mind and to accept a date with anyone else would have been cheating on Luke. Tracy's heart and mind were occupied with Luke. This led to a blurred reading of God's prompting. At that point, no one could come close to her heart.

"Say, what's wrong with two people spending time together? I mean, Luke probably protected her from some other jerk! What others think is their problem, not mine, right?" It may be difficult to explain because it is such a mental battle. Were their hearts pure? Did Tracy spend time with Luke because of the friendship or to continue her illusion that she and Luke might have a future together? Were the intentions of their friendship clear? Did they remain emotionally whole for their mates?

In all of your friendships with members of the opposite sex can you openly say to each person, "This is where our friendship stands; we are just friends"? If you can't, then you need to reconsider the purpose of your friendship and whether your heart is in too deep. This defining of the purpose of your friendship should, ideally, come from the man in any situation. Just as Christ is the initiator and humans are the responders, so too is the man the initiator and a woman the responder.

Okay, so you men out there, when you read that Tracy's heart was "taken" you might have thought, "What! How could she get herself that wrapped up in Luke? What's her problem? She must have been really desperate." Again it comes back to the female heart. Here is some more insight on women that may help turn on some light bulbs. Women are, no matter how much some fight it, very emotional. "Okay, I definitely knew that!" you say. But it's the God-given ability in women to easily connect on an emotional level with a man that strengthens our marriages, not our friendships. Did you catch that? This capacity to attach our hearts effortlessly is to be the glue for our marriages, not friendships.

As discussed earlier, the Bible commands women to learn to love their husbands, as it commands husbands to love their wives. It states, "Older women . . . encourage younger women to love their husbands" (Titus 2:3,4). "Wives, be subject to your own husbands, as to the Lord" (Eph. 5:22). During the time of learning to love our husbands, the emotional connection is the glue that holds marriages together. I believe this is part of the reason a woman stays with a man who abuses her—her emotional connection is so strong it keeps her there. This emotional attachment creates a devotion that makes some women behave as if they threw common sense out the window.

Men, ask yourselves these questions: What level of devotion do you want from your wife? Do you want your wife to still hold a glimmer of devotion for Jimmy from her high school days? Do you want to know that your wife saved her heart for you, all of it for you, no one else? Remember a virtuous woman does her husband good *all* the days of her life, not just her married days (Prov. 31:12). When a woman is kept free from any friendship with emotional devotion, she is saving it all for you! Wow! That's cool stuff.

When a woman uses this emotional glue to hold male friendships together it will not have the same adhesiveness when she finally marries. Think about a post-it-note. The first time you use the note, it stays straight, the edges don't curl, it stays in place almost wherever you put it. After about ten uses how well does that post-it-note stick to any surface? Not well at all. It loses even more stickiness when you put it on a dusty surface. The more impure the surface, the less ability it has to fuse. It is the same with the emotions of a woman: the more she sticks to Mr. Wrong, the less available they are to stick to Mr. Right.

Men, to explain how deep this connection is, know that when you ask a girl out for coffee she could be planning your wedding, naming your kids, and designing your beautiful vacation home. I am not joking, this is really how women think. I have been guilty of this and the guy had no idea how adorable our kids were and how grand our vacation home would be. Please note that this doesn't necessarily mean the girl is stark raving desperate. She is just being an emotional woman, the way God created her.

The third error in Tracy and Luke's friendship was that they stroked each other's egos. Tracy paid female attention to Luke. What an ego booster, having a beautiful girl give you undivided attention. When Luke shared his thoughts, feelings and struggles with Tracy it was a great feeling of being connected. But without a clear definition of their relationship, someone was bound to get hurt.

Whelchel also touches on this issue in her book.

I also observed too often that many singles—yes, Christian singles—enjoy sending signals and then disowning them. After all, it's an ego trip to think that one or two people are "on your string," hoping you'll come their way sooner or later, even if they're not attractive to you.

It is easy for men and women to lose focus during those single years when a man or woman steps into their life, especially if God has not done the prompting. For Tracy and Luke, losing their focus happened without their even realizing.

We need to become friends with our singleness. The number one goal during this time is to fix oneself on loving God with all our heart, soul, mind, and strength. When you grow in your love for Him you will desire to conform yourself to Him. You will put aside your own wishes and start living for His. Being single will then be easier. It may not come overnight, but with prayer and much reading of His holy and pure Word, you will see that His ways are best for you.

This may be one of the biggest mental battles you will have. It takes perseverance and tenacity. You can't give up. You have to fight the good fight of faith. Repent of thinking that marriage will solve your problems. Learn to fall in love with God. Trust Him for everything. He cares about all the details of your life. God has answered so many of my little prayer requests that it's now easier to trust Him with the big things. We like to be our own masters, but God is the Master and He deserves that respect.

God wants you to have joy in your singleness and He wants you to know He's not going to keep you single a day longer than He plans. He wants us to use our time as singles to serve and enjoy Him and to focus on obeying and trusting Him. As the old hymn states "Trust and obey, for there is no other way, to be happy in Jesus, but to trust and obey." So true, so true!

Thought Questions:
1. In the e-mail from my friend Michelle, the advice her sister gave was, "to practice being selfless." What are ways you practice this element for marriage?
2. How could a "friend" take our focus off of serving and enjoying God?
3. Why should someone befriend their single years?

13

God's Classroom

How does a person, without being emotionally intimate, become friends with members of the opposite sex? Whenever I have shared the idea that one should remain emotionally pure and whole for their mate, that is the number one question in response.

With God's way you protect emotions that are to be freely given to His mate of choice for you. There is freedom in saving your emotions for your spouse and spending time in your single years in God's private classroom.

Some of you, chances are many of you, have been in an undefined emotional relationship. Most people have had a couple of these risky interactions. Let's look at some things to do that may help heal some of your battle wounds. We will examine things you can do while you are waiting on God for Him to reveal His will in your daily life and your future.

First, there's no easy cure for the wounded heart when it comes to healing from an emotional relationship. Time may be all you have. Sounds so cliché but time will mend the broken hearted. By time I mean what God heals that takes however long. Time has been the biggest factor in repairing my heart from undefined emotional relationships.

Second, you need to avoid spending any more emotions that should be saved. Assess your current relationships. Are they defined? Do you know whether you are future mates or just friends? Back away emotionally from any undefined relationship, or work toward defining it.

Backing off may be incredibly hard because your heart will tell you that backing away from this friendship is illogical. "I mean, this person is still my brother or sister in Christ, right? How could I be so rude?" you may ask. But if this "rudeness" is protection then it is not rudeness; it is guarding your heart. Guarding your heart is what God calls us to do in Proverbs 4:23: "Above all else, guard your heart for it is the wellspring of life." If you don't guard your heart those wellsprings may come pouring from your teary eyes, not your heart.

Let's look at our current culturally accepted way of relationships. You get to know someone they don't like you the way you like them; heart pain results. Meet someone new; get to know them, a little more guarded this time; you don't really like them the way they like you; you break their heart. Meet another potential mate; get to know each other, even more guarded, maybe a little bit cynical; both like each other; get physically intimate; break up. You meet yet another person; stay really guarded emotionally; know in your heart this is God's mate for you, but the chance of heart pain is too great to risk the commitment. Hmmm, so my suggestion for "rudeness" ends the cycle, that doesn't sound too bad after all.

Nathaniel and Andrew Ryun stated this as clearly as one can in their book *It's a Lifestyle: Discipleship in Our Relationships*.

Emotions are given away, hearts tied together, and then torn apart. Emotions and feelings are trampled with impunity . . . This continual giving of emotions, and then separating, leaves wounds that can last for years and prove a tough obstacle to overcome in marriage. The "hearts" given away in marriage are not much more than bruised illusions of healthy and whole hearts.

If you decide that stepping away from a relationship is God's best for your heart and emotions, then it will be a call to wholehearted obedience. When I struggled in an undefined emotional relationship I fasted from him. What do I mean by "fasted from him"? Well, I stopped seeing him, which was hard because we lived at the same campus. I did not go out of my way to talk to him. I did not manipulate situations to see him. I basically avoided him. You know what he did? Nothing. It did not even faze him. This was a big clue for me. Fasting from him was one of the smartest things I did. I thank God for His insight. Though it did not cure me of having feelings for the guy, it did put our relationship into perspective.

The choice is yours. The other thing you could do is define your relationship. Be bold enough to ask politely where you stand. What are his or her intentions? Don't be afraid of ending your fantasy. Any time you spend thinking about or being with that person, you are wasting time you could spend finding and developing a relationship with your future mate. Your future mate may be watching you but perhaps thinks you're "a couple" in that undefined relationship.

Dealing with relationship baggage will look different for each of you. Pray that God will show you what He wants you to do. Dealing with any baggage before you walk down the aisle will enhance the success of your marriage. If relational rubbish is not dealt with before the "I do's," then one or both partners may be so into self-gratification that the marriage will not be honoring to God, or the marriage will be focused horizontally, not vertically.

Let's remember that contentment is not the "gift" of celibacy, nor is it the magic key that gives God the go ahead to send a spouse your way. Being content does not mean giving up hope. So, once you have come to a place where you are content with God's plan for your life and you strive to have an undistracted devotion to Him, how do you enroll in God's classroom?

First, continue to seek Him with all you have. For most of us, this is a *moment-by-moment* choice we must make. It requires dying to your will. Dying to what we want and replacing it with what God wants. This is the hardest part of obedience. Our wills are stubborn, and we have become good at avoiding the act of allowing our hearts to be molded into the image of Christ. Who are we to decide what to allow God to change or not to change?

Second, you want to make sure you are serving Him. This will look different for each one of us. Look at the time that you have and ask the Lord to show where you need to serve.

One mistake to avoid when looking to serve is trying to minister where you are not called. Keeping yourself busy with lots of ministries will not satisfy, but serving where He wants you is tremendously rewarding. When you are seeking Him first He can do awesome things and open doors of ministry you thought were impossible.

When God's Spirit leads you in ministry, it may look completely different than what you imagine. Ministering for God's kingdom is poles apart from our preconceived ideas.

The third thing to do is to make yourself emotionally unavailable to the opposite sex. Do I mean buy a wedding ring and pretend you are married? Of course not! I mean keep yourself away from situations in which your heart can be drawn to a person and possibly take your focus off the Lord. Have you ever thought about how God feels when you give attention, time, thoughts, and emotions to another human and not to Him? "For your husband is your Maker" (Isa. 54:5a). If you saw God as your mate, how jealous would He be over you?

When you think of God as your spouse, then it seems to put some things into perspective. When we pray from the selfishness of our hearts for a mate, it can be compared to going to your spouse and asking for money for a prostitute because your spouse is not satisfying you. This is unheard of and absolutely vulgar, but that is what we are doing when we ask God to satisfy our fleshly desires for a mate.

"You ask and you do not receive, because you ask with wrong motives, so that you may spend it on your own pleasures" (James 4:3).

As I have looked back over my journals, I see times that I placed myself in situations where I could easily be emotionally intimate with men. I would pray with them, spend one-on-one time with them, tell them my pains, and share dreams and hopes with them. My heart was deceiving me. I thought I could be around them and not step over the line of emotional and spiritual intimacy. I could not. My heart was left unprotected.

As I said earlier, my heart has bumps and bruises on it, and my desire is to see others learn from some of my mistakes. God revealed something big to me about the time I would spend with single guys. One guy, with whom I shared a deep emotional connection, married a couple of years ago. When I found out he was getting married the thought came to me, "Every time we were alone, praying, talking, sharing, and laughing his future wife and my future husband were sitting right between us." Whoa! God hit me over the head with that one! I looked back and saw how conversations and actions would have been completely avoided had this been our mindset.

Personally, I have learned to not place myself in situations where my heart might be drawn to an unmarried man. I have a tendency to start imagining things that are not there and before I know it—of course, this can take all of two minutes—my mind is off in La La Land of Marriage. Can this be hard to avoid? Yes! Does it go completely against the flow of the world? Yes! Does God sustain me? Yes!

The fourth action that can be taken is to ask God to enroll you in His "Wife or Husband Training Program." The Holy Spirit is our teacher, and if you know deep in your heart that your desire to be married is from the Lord, then ask Him to prepare you.

We go to college for four years or more to prepare for a profession, yet most people do not prepare for the life role that will influence generations to come. Mull over in your mind the fact that when you enter into a marriage you are, Lord willing, going to create a child, an eternal, forever, timeless, everlasting being. How much time have you put into preparing to guide, lead, and develop that child for the kingdom of God? That, in and of itself, is powerful and should not be taken lightly.

Preparing to be married will look different for men and for women. I would like to make some suggestions on things both can do to prepare for marriage and life.

Men, although I am a woman, God has given me some comprehension on the roles of a husband and these points could help.

1. Start praying for your wife and family. Your prayers as a husband will greatly affect how you treat your wife (1 Pet. 3:9). Covering your wife and family in prayers now will bring a great reaping later. You will reap the benefits or consequences of what you sow.

2. Practice being a leader. Most men, in the flesh, are followers. They would rather go with the flow and follow a leader. As a husband, you are required by God to lead your family (Eph. 5:23). When you lead your family, God receives the glory because in your flesh you desire to follow. Therefore you are leading in your weakness. This, in turn, glorifies God. "'My grace is sufficient for you, for power is perfected in weakness.' Most gladly, therefore, I will rather boast about my weaknesses, so that the power of Christ may dwell in me" (2 Cor. 12:9). God not only asks you to lead, but also to be a servant leader as Christ is to the church. Serving your mom, sisters, and brothers will help you gain a better understanding of what this service is to look like. I would recommend that you do not try to learn to be a leader with a godly sister in Christ, unless your relationship is clearly defined. To a woman this can be confusing. God can show you areas in which to lead before you are married that will benefit your wife and family.

3. Ask God to teach you what it means to protect your wife and family. Protection means not only from the elements and harmful situations, but also to protect your wife's heart. As we have seen throughout this book, a woman has a sensitive heart. Her emotions and feelings are to be sheltered from the elements of the world. This means that you, as the man, will have to stick your neck out and be willing to accept success or failure.

God has been teaching my dad on this issue, and it is a key to a healthy marriage. When my dad takes ownership of a situation it frees my mom to feel emotionally protected. For example, my dad checked into a hotel. The room was smoky and they wanted a non-smoking room. What did he do? Well, he does not like conflict; he told my mom they would stay put. Now, my mom is a great leader. After asking my dad if she could handle the situation, she picked up the phone, called the front desk and they changed to a non-smoking room. My dad did not protect my mom. He allowed her to do the confrontation so that his ego could be protected. *When the outcome of a situation is not known a man will protect his ego before he will protect his wife's emotions.*

My father really started understanding this type of protection when they began home educating. He told my mom, "I want you to home school and I take full responsibility for success or failure of this decision." This freed up my mom to have more emotions and love to give the family.

During one of my girl friend's engagement stage, I took time to prod her with questions. One question was whether she planned on working after they had kids. She said she didn't know if she would or not but, either way, her future husband was behind her decision 100 percent. Some may say, "What a supportive husband." I say, "No, he's not supportive at all." Down the road let's say my friend chooses to work and she is totally and completely stressed out. What is her husband's responsibility in the matter? None! His out: "Well, it was your choice to work." Therefore he is not taking on the success or failure of her working. His ego is protected and his wife's heart is not.

As a woman, I desire my husband to protect me emotionally so that I have more love to bestow upon him. My father is my protector now and the more emotionally free I am, the more love and tenderness I have to give. It is a beautiful thing. A man's ability to protect his wife in all areas will greatly enhance the quality of his marriage.

4. Prepare your home. How I would love to marry a man who has been saving money for marriage. When a single guy spends money foolishly he is taking away money from his future wife and family. Most of you will have a family; you just don't have it now. My friend Bob saved money for his wife and family since he was seven. When he approached marriage he had money to buy a nice ring, pay for their honeymoon and still have money for a down payment on a condo. He thought ahead and did not live in the moment.

Adapting these few points for your life will better equip you to be a godly husband and a man who has his heart directly hooked up to the heart of the Father.

Women, our role as wives will affect generations to come. We have lost sight of how influential God created women to be. When we strive to obtain power over a man, we leave no room for the man to be a man, thus we lose our ability to influence. We feel frustrated and hurt. There are some things that I have learned to do in order to prepare to be a wife. It is not easy! It goes against nature and only through God's goodness can we ever learn these things.

1. Pray for your husband now. A wife who prays for her husband is a powerful tool for the Kingdom of Heaven. As for me, I have been faithfully praying for my husband since 1996. Each year has a different focus and it will be awesome to see God bring those prayer requests to completion when He chooses.

2. Learn submission. Women, in our flesh we are leaders, willing to take on whatever conflicts are necessary to mend a situation. When we submit and follow, we are doing so through the grace of God. Coming under the authority of man is not easy for most women. We live in a

culture that tells you this type of submission is irrational and ludicrous. That's why there are so many books out there about this topic. Nowhere does Scripture say that a woman is not under some form of authority.

> But I want you to understand that Christ is the head of every man, and the man is the head of *every* woman and God is the head of Christ (1 Cor. 11:2 emphasis added).

Women and men misunderstand submission. Because of this common misunderstanding, we tend to put up our defenses and let our independent spirits take over. As a woman, you have to admit we can be feisty, and that quality can be used for a greater good or used to tear apart a family. "The wise woman builds her house, but the foolish tears it down with her own hands" (Prov. 14:1).

When we as women truly understand submission, our lives will flow at a much smoother pace. Often we do not submit because we feel the process is taking a bit too long. This is the number one reason I struggle with submitting to my father. I make decisions much faster than he does. Does it mean that my decisions are better than his? No. Whatever the reasons, I am called to submit to my father, and then my husband, at their pace and give them space to allow the Holy Spirit to bring about what is the best in the situation.

Also, when we submit and allow a husband to lead in a godly fashion we obey the order God has established. God's order of authority is God, man, woman. So when we come under the authority of a husband we are under God's authority. Men like to be appreciated and be respected. Ephesians 5:33b states, "The wife must see to it that she respects her husband." Respecting your husband will include honoring his decisions and his timing, as well as allowing him the freedom to know he can trust that his mate will not lose heart when he has to take a step of faith with areas in your marriage and life. With the support of a wife, a man can be successful. Like the old saying goes, "Behind every good man is a good woman." When respect and submission are channeled in a godly way, men are freed to be that servant leader in all areas of their life, work, home, and church.

Submitting does not include manipulation. We become very good at manipulating situations to obtain what we want. This can be dangerous, because no matter the outcome, true satisfaction will not occur. We have a great deal of influence over men and that must be kept in God's will and not used for selfish gain.

Learning to submit before the "I do's" will greatly lessen the pain of learning submission after marriage.

3. Let your husband protect your emotions, so you are free to be the "love" givers of the family. This emotional tenderness God gave us is to be used to provide an atmosphere in our homes that is warm and inviting. When we don't let a husband protect our emotions we have less emotion to give a husband and family. The way I see it, we are to be the "love makers" in the family, making home a place where a husband will want to come to after work, not a place filled with battles, disorder and headaches.

As we discussed earlier, men have egos and do not like conflict when the outcome is unknown. As wives, we must learn to provide an environment in which a husband is free to speak—ramification-free. I have seen men keep their mouths shut at meetings or social groups because of what their wives may say on the drive home. You know what I am talking about here. What husband wants the wait-till-we-get-home attitude? No man I know feels free to express himself with that type of wife.

Learning to be protected will go against everything in you. Protection is becoming to a woman of any age. Ask God to teach you what protection looks like during your unmarried years. Again, it is the line of authority God set up!

4. Prepare your home. Wait, didn't I say that to the men? Yes, I did. But for women it may look different. I live at home with my parents, and so most of the items I use belong to them. So I have begun my own collection. Ever heard of the term "hope chest"? I think the idea of a hope chest is a wonderful thing. I expect to enter into a marriage with basic items already purchased. Being ready to set up a home will prepare you for the mental and emotional changes that will take place within the first years of marriage.

I explained to a married girlfriend of mine how I feel it is important for me to prepare tangibly for marriage. Over the phone I could almost feel her look of, "Huh?" Then she sweetly asked, "Well, Heather, are you dating anyone?" "No," I replied, feeling somewhat stupid. Then the conversation carried on to other things. She and her husband had longed for a child and God did not open her womb. In a matter of two weeks they adopted a little boy. She told me how chaotic her house was upon the arrival of their son. Then a light bulb went off in my head. I said, "That is why I am preparing for marriage. Most people have nine months to prepare for a child. I do not know how long I have to prepare for marriage, so I am getting ready. I want to step smoothly into my marriage." Thinking she had plenty of time to prepare for a baby, my friend had an "aha moment!"

Preparing your home may go beyond buying tangible items. It would include mentally preparing what type of home you want. Not necessarily the style like country or Victorian, but how do you want people to *feel* when they walk into your home? My parents had a vision when they built the house we currently live in. Part of that vision was to construct a home that is warm, inviting, and cozy. I believe they succeeded. Most people say that when they hit the first step to our country style wrap-around porch they feel like they are coming home.

Being able to have a smooth transition into marriage—emotionally, spiritually, and physically—will provide a calm, peaceful life. Again, preparing oneself for marriage will be a blessing for both parties.

5. Women, we need to stop treating men like they are our husbands. We are created with a nature that longs to serve and please a man, but when we do this, we take away *their* desire for a wife. I have seen single girls fuss over who is going to serve a guy his coffee. Really, let him get it himself if your motives are not pure. Let's not misuse serving to satisfy a longing for a husband. Also, if women are giving men companionship outside of marriage he will never be hungry for it. Women have the ability to create a "void" in a man's life, so that we will become self-motivated to fill it with the presence of a wife. It's a new twist on the old saying, "playing hard to get."

Let's recap. Gentlemen, are you being prepared to take responsibility for a wife and a family by the lifestyle you are living now? Are you learning what it means to protect and provide for your wife? Does a carefree lifestyle prepare you to be a godly husband?

Women, does your flirtatious attitude make you ready to settle down to one man? When you open up emotionally with a man, are you giving away emotions that are to be saved for your future mate? Are you learning now what it means to be submissive and have a quiet and gentle spirit? Can you effectively and smoothly run a house and make it a haven of peace and love?

How much time have we wasted thus far? When we are in our single years we must realize that, most likely, we will have a family. We may not be able to see them, but we must make decisions today that will positively affect them later.

Men and women need to search Scripture and ask God to show them what qualities He wants in a godly husband or wife. For me personally, God has shown me what a quiet and gentle spirit is to look like. When I think of someone with a quiet and gentle spirit I envision someone who is able to take whatever life tosses their way with peace and joy. They do not seek to serve their own needs. They have power perfectly blended with seasoned self-control.

God asks men to lead their families as Christ leads the church (Eph. 5:23), and women to be submissive to their husbands (Eph. 5:22). The relationship of a husband protecting and providing for his wife, and a wife being submissive to her husband's authority is beautiful. It is the way that God intended it to be, so what is not lovely about it?

If we are not preparing ourselves for marriage we can experience frustration when expectations are not met. I have seen newly married men who do not protect their wives, feeling suffocated by the new commitment. I see new brides who flirt with other guys and have a hard time communicating with their new husbands. This is a shame and it should open our eyes to see that these ways are not most effective.

When you walk down the aisle, do you want to be a groom who does not know what it means to protect and provide for your bride? Brides, do you want to be presented as stubborn and independent wives? The time is now while you are single, to learn how to be what God wants you to be.

Let God train you, and if that means He brings in older adults or your parents into your life, then submit yourself to Him. He knows what is best and during this season of singleness present yourself as a living sacrifice and wait on our holy Father. This is pleasing in His sight.

Remaining fixed on His plan and His friendship during these years will save you and your mate a great deal of pain. His ways are far better than anything we could do on our own!

Thought Questions:
1. Would stepping away from an undefined emotional relationship help with someone's spiritual life? How?
2. Do you need some training in the Husband/Wife Training Program? What type of training?
3. What "classes" would you add to the Training Program?

14

My Dating Alternative

Some of you may wonder how I plan to get married. That could be another book, so please bear with my *"Reader's Digest"* version. Also, please know that this dating alternative is what God has led our family to do. His spirit may lead you down a completely different-*looking* path, but the heart of the matter is that we are striving to please Him with purity in all areas.

My faith is completely resting on God to provide a mate for me. I trust that He is preparing a mate for me and me for a mate. It is my faith that casts away any doubt. I have asked God for certain qualities in a husband, and I have to be patient while God works on my mate's heart. When these qualities are answered, I will know beyond a shadow of a doubt this is the right man for me. Do you think God is going to say, "Oh no, I forgot to introduce Heather to her husband! I guess she will be single the rest of her life." Hardly. I know I will not remain single a day longer than God wants me to be.

Before I get practical, I would ask you to remove any preconceived ideas you have about the Christian dating scene or even what you think I am telling you. Read carefully. This is what I believe God has called me to do. You need to be pure and that may take a different shape for you than for me. The Jews had their own preconceived idea of the Messiah, and when He came they did not recognize Him. Try your best not to limit God.

The first part of this alternative dating is to have the total involvement of my family in my process toward marriage. My sisters hold me accountable and help me avoid the pitfalls of premature emotional intimacy.

My parents give me guidance and advice, along with protecting my heart. My parents have my heart (Prov. 23:26 states that God wants us to give our parents our hearts) and I trust them with it. I have turned my heart to my father and he has turned his heart to me. Malachi 4:6a states, "He [God] will restore the hearts of the fathers to their children and the hearts of the children to their fathers." My mother and father have loved me from before I was born and have cared for me more than any other human being. I see my father as an active participant in helping me make the right choice in a mate. Does that mean he is a control freak and wants to dictate everything I do? No. He sees my heart and, just like my heavenly Father, he wants what is best for me.

Unfortunately, I believe that many women have not experienced a man in their life who has had their best interests at heart; so, this type of submission is hard to understand. So many people have been hurt and abused that this level of trust seems nearly impossible, but nothing is too difficult for God. He can heal and restore your heart in ways no one can even fathom. My prayer for anyone who doesn't have a solid relationship with their father, is either that they will be able to repair that relationship or find an older Christian couple to help in this process. I see both of my fathers, heavenly and earthly, helping me avoid intimacy before commitment.

Since intimacy and commitment go hand and hand, when the man I am to marry comes along God already will have been preparing him for me. I pray we will get to know each other around our families and will see each other's true colors before any commitment is made. As I said, I rarely spend extended one-on-one time with any man except my father, so to know me my future husband will have to learn about me around other people, mostly my family. Also, I have asked God to work a miracle in the situation. He can protect me from becoming emotional before the time He ordains it. I pray that, with the wisdom of my parents, I will make a wise choice.

Some of you are asking, "Did this girl have a Brady Bunch life? I would never, ever want my parents involved in my choice of who I marry!" No, my life was not the script of a TV show, but I do trust my parents. If you do not have this trust relationship with your parents, then I encourage you to pray that God will repair any broken relationships with your parents or bring into your life some older, wiser Christians who desire to guide you. Seek advice from someone you trust and allow yourself to come under his or her authority.

An older friend of mine and I talked about this issue. She was not raised in a Christian home, and so looking toward her mother and stepfather for guidance was a ridiculous thought when she was younger. Through studying the Word and hearing godly advice, she decided that her decision to give up a well-established career at age 29 in order to Bible college needed the blessing of her stepfather, a non-believer.

God arranged their meeting time perfectly and she laid her plans before him. She had purposed in her heart that whatever he said she would obey. After explaining the pros and cons, her heart behind the matter, and her plans, she waited for her stepfather's answer. "That sounds like a good idea, your career will be waiting for you when you are done," was his response. She had his blessing.

As she looks over this pivotal event in her life, she sees how God showed her that, whether or not her stepfather was a believer, she was still to honor him. At Bible college she met her future husband and today their marriage is truly a picture of Christ and His church. Her career was waiting for her—being a wife and mother. But it was waiting at college not back at home.

God asks us to take a leap of faith by giving up our full control in finding a mate. God can do anything He wants. He is rich, powerful, well networked, and ready to bless His obedient children. Who wouldn't want Him to find you a mate? I mean, can you imagine how big his "little black book" is! He's the ultimate dating service!

God has set up roles when it comes to the steps we take toward marriage. Proverbs 18:22 says, "He who finds a wife, finds a good thing and obtains favor from the Lord." So the way I see it, I am to be found, not to be out looking myself. Whenever someone asks my sister where she is going to find her husband, she always responds, "Is he lost?"

The man's role is going to be different. As the Proverb states, "He who finds a wife . . ." the man is to do the finding and the initiating. My prayer is that any man looking for a wife would be willing to come under the submission of his father or an older Christian man. Again, Christ is the example a man is to follow. Christ is the initiator, not the church. When women are aggressive they leave no room for the man to be the initiator, which sets a tone for the relationship.

Paul wrote some wonderful advice to Timothy (a young man) on how to treat a younger woman, "as a sister, in all purity" (1 Tim. 5:2). In Greek the word "all" is *pas*, meaning to all things individually and in their totality. A man must treat a younger woman in all purity. How does a brother treat his sister? I do not have any brothers, but I know that in most family situations the brothers and sisters do not pay attention to one over the other, communicating feelings of "you're special;" nor do they step over any lines of physical intimacy. They also have no hidden agendas. Where they stand with each other is clear. Now, do brothers and sisters know each other? Yes. Do they care for one another? Yes. Do they love each other? Well, I hope so. Then what is Paul talking about? Paul stated that all women a man comes in contact with must be treated with all purity. Only God can give the green light to take a relationship to another level of intimacy. When God gives the green light, purity remains in its proper place.

Some of you may say Luke treated Tracy as a sister, but did he really? He set her apart, made her feel special and, without even knowing it, he took over her thought life. In a physical sense he did treat her purely, but what about her emotions? He was not up-front with his intentions. If he had been, she might not have allowed herself to become worked up over him. Tracy did allow herself to become worked up over Luke, so you cannot put all the blame on him. They had a closeness, but no commitment. He was taking away emotions that should have been saved for her husband.

A friend of mine who works at a college shared with me his insight on how the male/female relationships are loose, with very few limits. There are no boundaries and guidance in this issue. I wholeheartedly agreed with him and after giving it some thought, I concluded we have all become calloused when it comes to being sensitive toward how we are to treat our brothers and sisters in Christ.

Have you ever felt the hands of a seasoned guitar player, gardener, construction worker, or quilter? They are often well calloused and those callouses can withstand a great deal of abuse before the person feels any pain. So is the human heart when it becomes calloused. The buildup of hard, rough insensitive layers must be cut through before any pain is felt. Then when pain is eventually felt, the cut is deep. With loose male/female relationships the heart can withstand a great deal of pain, because it has lost the sense of feeling. A re-sensitized heart may actually feel less pain because of its early detection mechanism.

The husband is the head of the wife and that means he is responsible for sticking his neck out and being held accountable. When an unmarried man sticks his neck out with a young lady, he is preparing himself for the role God has assigned to him in his marriage. Christ put His life on the line, with no guarantee that we would respond. What a great life lesson men can learn in taking the initiative in relationships.

As I move on to another level of getting to know each other, my father will be involved. After the young man passes the "dad test" we will then be in the getting-to-know-each-other process. This interested young man will spend time with my father long before he spends one-on-one time with me. My father and he will get to know each other intimately, before he and I get to know each other intimately. During this time my father can objectively view this young man's qualities. My dad already knows what qualities I desire in a mate, so he will see how this young man measures up. As they say, "love is blind," so before there is even a chance of me "falling in love," my dad will screen the young man. If he is not the right one, then my heart will be spared the pain of intimacy without a commitment. (Of course I know that God's plan for my marriage may *look* totally different than even this path. I am willing to obey whatever steps He calls me to.)

With people around us, I will not be as prone to share and discuss things that I should not. When other people are present conversation is not allowed to flow in whatever direction it chooses. We will both be protected emotionally from stepping over lines that must be saved for after a commitment. This does not mean that my family is going to listen to every phone call or screen every e-mail. But it does mean that my heart is protected and I do not have to put my heart out there to be devoured or hurt. There is freedom in all of this and I pray that you will not see this as legalistic.

An example of my dad's involvement came in January 1999. I was an emcee at a Christian conference. A group of women wanted a top-ten list I had written. I asked if they had an e-mail address. They did not, but a man in their group did. They sent this young, single guy my way and we exchanged e-mail addresses. Later that week I e-mailed him the list.

Several nights later, I was on-line and he instant-messaged me (this is where you can chat with someone on the computer). We chatted for a while. I told my dad that he seemed nice and I asked dad to check it out. Dad sent him an e-mail asking him about his intentions toward me. Soon after that the young man wrote my dad back and stated he had a girlfriend.

Now, how was this freedom? I was protected from offering any emotions without a commitment. What if we had kept writing each other and if we became friends over e-mail? Knowing me, I would have become emotionally tangled with him, thinking maybe this is "the one," only to find out he had a girlfriend. This saved me from doing any of that. Being free to save those emotions is wonderful, or as Martha Stewart would say, "It's a good thing!"

A little crazy? Sure, but I am thankful I saved myself— and him for that matter—any further hurt. Knowing I have this protective covering over me allows me to serve and focus on God and Him alone.

I have an important role as well in protecting my heart. As I mentioned, I rarely spend alone time with men and this is not something I have always believed. When I was in college I had a guy friend and we would spend hours alone. Because I never had romantic feelings in his direction, spending time with him was enjoyable. As I worked on this book I got back in touch with him, after not seeing him for three years. He wanted to do some shopping. I used to spend a great deal of time with this guy, so what do I do? Prior to this I did not care about the time spent alone with him, but now I want to protect myself. So my sister decided to go with us. Now, she did not follow us or even listen to every conversation, but she helped me obey the call God has on my life. My role is to find a way to enjoy this friendship without the possibilities of elevating it to an emotional level.

What did our day look like? My sister and I went to the mall. We had three hours to shop and she went one way and I waited for Jake. When he came, we began to make our way through hundreds of shoppers. About two hours into our shopping, we met up with my sister and finished our shopping. So was it the time limit, the public interaction and knowing that my sister was there that kept my heart pure? No, it was my desire to serve God through my personal purity.

Again, this process is going to look different for each one of us. You may not need to take your sister along, but for me, it allowed me to see my friend without worrying about my heart. It all boils down to the heart of each one of us. A couple may be out alone and have completely pure hearts. Then another couple could have impure motives and be in a large group of people. The way the Spirit leads will take different forms for each of us. God asks us to guard our hearts and not to defraud one another. How that manifests itself is between you and the Lord.

Emotional purity will take on many forms, and the stories below are all ways that my friends' personal purity played out.

First, there are Scott and Anne. Their first meeting occurred overseas during an extended mission trip. They were still young and not looking for mates. They were just acquaintances at the time and had mutual friends. It wasn't until a few years later that their friendship was rekindled when Scott worked with Anne's brother-in-law. Anne then had the chance to "get to know" Scott around her family, and thus was attracted to his godliness, personality, and character.

Unknown to one another, the Lord began to draw their hearts to each other as the Lord placed them in circumstances and situations together. Neither one let the other know what feelings were there.

When Scott realized he wanted to pursue a relationship with marriage in mind, he talked to Anne's father. Anne's father and Scott spent time in an "interviewing" process and Scott shared about his intentions toward Anne and what God had done in his heart to draw him to her. Anne's father gave Scott permission to then share his heart with Anne, and see what God would do.

Because of what God had done in Anne's heart, it didn't take too long for the two of them to know this was God's will for them. They spent time together getting to know each other on a more intimate level. Many questions were asked and answered, time was spent with each other's families and friends. God confirmed during this time that they were for each other. Ten months later they were married. No one can question that Scott and Anne were created for each other.

The next couple is Sam and Pam. When Pam was twelve her father died. Her mother expected her to live and think with complete independence as a young adult, withholding advice even when Pam dared to request it. As a college senior, she unwisely dated a man who eventually brought an enormous amount of stress, turmoil, and pain into her life. It was the severe trial of that dating relationship that led her to realize how little wisdom she had. She fervently prayed that no other man would pursue her until she had experienced an incredible growth in wisdom. Six years passed.

At Pam's church, which had no singles ministry, she had become acquainted with Sam under *no* pretense of being attracted to one another. For more than a year they interacted as would any members of their friendly church— no romantic ties and not even a hint of flirtation. So when Sam expressed an interest in Pam, she did not believe him initially. Because he was a few years younger than she, she did not think that he was really ready for a permanent relationship. She asked Sam to seek counseling from their pastor before she felt at peace with his pursuit. Sam followed through with her request, much to Pam's surprise, and came under the accountability of their pastor in order to date

Pam. Six month's later they became engaged. Throughout most of their engagement they met with their pastor weekly. After fourteen years of marriage, Sam and Pam still reap the benefits of their pastor's protection and involvement.

Do you have a better sense of how emotional purity can look for you? Both of these couples remained emotionally pure and both have such different stories.

Remaining emotionally pure for my mate is exciting. I can't wait to be not only physically pure for him, but emotionally pure. I have faith that these protective measures I am taking will enhance my marriage. Purity is beautiful. Holiness should be desired. The blessings that come from striving toward purity and holiness do not compare to the short-term emotional gratification one may receive.

Another blessing from my dating alternative is I will know that my marriage was not based on me using *anything* to attract a young man's attention. I will always know that he initiated the relationship, and the respect that comes from that is irreplaceable. He will be sure that I responded unconditionally to his initiating. There will never be the "does-he/she-like-me" uncertainty. There will be no silly questioning of our intentions with each other. I will never have to turn to the daisy and ask, "Does he love me? Does he love me not?" In the long run this will lay a foundation of trust and respect in our marriage. Who could ask for anything more wonderful than that?

If you feel completely insensitive in this matter of male/female relationships, ask God to pull away some of those calloused layers and make you tender to the boundaries He would have for you.

> Moreover, I will give you a new heart and put a new spirit within you; and I will remove the heart of stone from your flesh and give you a heart of flesh. I will put

My Spirit within you and cause you to walk in My stat-
utes, and you will be careful to observe My ordinances
(Ezek. 36:26-27).

When I worked in ministry in Denver I signed a
contract that I would not watch R-rated movies for one
year. You know what happened? I became very sensitive to
the content of movies, even to the point that most PG-13
movies are shocking and undesirable to me. I became
resensitized to what is pure, lovely, and of good repute.

Most people ask for solid answers to these tough
questions, but we must realize that when our hearts and
motives are pure, our actions will manifest themselves in
that direction. As you seek God, serve Him, and focus on
Him as you would a spouse, watch and see what awesome
things only He can do!

Thought Questions:
1. Would my dating alternative benefit in your life? If
so, how?
2. What is God speaking to you regarding your dating
life?
3. What are ways you might protect yourself from
becoming emotionally intimate with someone?

15

God Created Marriage

he Lord God said, "It is not good for the man to be alone; I will make him a helper suitable for him" (Gen. 2:18). I'm sure most of you have heard the joke—probably many times over—that tells how God created man, saw He could do better, and so He created woman. This one usually registers about an eight on the laugh-o-meter, with women laughing most heartily, though it is not really funny. Upon deeper inspection of God's Word, and with an awareness of God's basis for creating males and females, we will uncover a better understanding of our purpose and function as unmarried people.

Why did God create marriage? Was it for friendship, companionship, love, to populate the earth? Or was it so He could watch us struggle with not having something we want? What was Adam doing before Eve? Why did God institute marriage and why should the path toward marriage maintain consistency with His plan?

God created man and saw that he did not have a suitable helpmate. Adam was keeping busy in the garden, working and enjoying fellowship with *Elohim* (Creator Lord).

He was just minding his own business, naming the animals (Gen. 2:19). Adam had uninterrupted communion with Jehovah when God said to him in Genesis 2:18a, "It is not good for man to be alone." God saw that Adam needed a counterpart or helper, and this person was to be a blessing in his life. Wow! God created a person especially for Adam, one who would be one flesh with him and would be fitting to his needs.

In *The Power of Femininity Rediscovering the Art of Being a Woman*, Michelle McKinney Hammond puts it bluntly.

> God had a brilliant idea! . . . Poor thing, this creature needed help. God had given him a lot of work to do, and He realized that Adam needed help staying focused on it. He would need extra encouragement from time to time. He needed someone to fill in the blanks, take up the slack, keep him together. He needed a "helpmate," a partner – someone designed especially to complement him in every way. This person would add dimension to his life, would be strong where he was weak. This person, called woman, would assist him in completing his assignment to subdue, maintain order, cultivate and take care of God's creation, to be fruitful and multiply. These things he could not do without her help.

I often find it amazing that Adam had such a beautiful, *distraction-free* relationship with God, yet God found it "good" for a woman to be his companion. God created woman to be a helper for man. Some women may have their noses bent out of shape when the Bible says they were created for man. But after God stated, "It's not good for man to be alone," He said, "I will make him a helper suitable for him" (Gen. 2:18b). Paul reinforced this wonderful purpose for women in 1 Corinthians 11:8, 9, "For man does not originate from woman, but woman from man; for indeed man was not created for the woman's sake, but woman for the man's sake."

Fortified with this knowledge, we women should feel honored to be qualified for such an important position. Men need us! While sitting in the large medical recliner, I was telling my dentist about my book project, that I was in the middle of writing a book on singles. Since he's been married for more than 35 years I decided to ask for his opinion on being single. He answered laughingly, "Don't get married." Then, just as quickly, he added, "No, us men need you women."

Since women were created to be a helpmate for man, why does the desire for marriage surprise women? Why does the desire for a home of our own shock us? Why does it anger others? Why do others deny or surpress it? We have lost sight of the beautiful role a woman plays in a man's life. God created us to serve and work along side a man. This natural, God-given longing is to be treasured; yet many of us perceive it as a burden we must bear. Some say that our "equal rights" are not being respected. We must look at everything through God's perspective, not what the world is telling us.

Desiring to be a wife or a husband is what God has put in the hearts of many of His children. He longs to show off through our marriages. However, when we allow our own selfish desires to take root, His goodness and mercies cannot shine through. Adam and Eve were put together to demonstrate Christ's lordship and the church's submission.

God, in His boundless love and grace, longs for us to know His love for us. To know the sacrifices He was willing to make so that one day we might be with Him forever is amazing. He knows us well. He created us. He knows we are programmed to understand word pictures. Think about all the prophets, the parables and His own Son's death on the cross; they all paint pictures of God's heart. God is the most-handsome, most powerful being and He made Himself invisible so we would follow Him, based not on looks or riches, but on love. He uses the daily rotation of the earth to illustrate the idea of His new mercies each morning. The snow is used in the Bible to represent the whiteness of our sins when we have been washed with Jesus' blood (Isa. 1:18). Hosea presents one of the most well-defined word pictures in the Bible. God asked Hosea to marry a prostitute to show Israel's unfaithfulness. One can fully understand the heart of a husband whose wife has a wandering heart. He also uses marriage to paint a picture.

He created marriage to mirror our relationship to Him and the love He has for us. We, the church, are the bride and Jesus is the bridegroom. In the book of Revelation, John more than once describes Jesus as the bridegroom (Rev. 19:7, 21:2,9). That marriage will take place and the bride (the church) must prepare herself for the bridegroom.

He longs for marriages to point people to Him. He wants the glory He deserves. When you understand that you have a link to the Father, through Jesus His Son, an amazing thing takes place. God knocks on the door to your heart and then He wants to dine with you (Rev. 3:20). He receives the credit. It is not on our account that we are let into the presence of God.

When one is considering marriage, certain questions must be asked: Will this marriage point people to the Father? Will this marriage honor Him above all else? This is His reason for marriage. He created marriage to show off His love, His perfect love. When two believers marry, they must lay aside selfish desires and know that God will use the love they have for each other to show others the love of the Father. This is an awesome responsibility and should not be taken with even a hint of selfishness. A marriage of two believers should be so drastically different than that of two non-believers that the world should crave what we have—God's love. Marriage is one of God's evangelistic tools.

When we think about our pre-Christ life, we can see the dramatic difference His love has made. Many of you laid aside old sinful behaviors and became new creatures in Him. If you think about it, your commitment to Christ was made with little knowledge of what was to come, right? You may look back and think, "How did I get here?" The trials and pain, joy and excitement, are all a part of getting to know God, but did you know that when you started? Most of us who know the Lord never could imagine what our loving God would do for us. The same is true for marriage.

The beginning of Tracy and Luke's relationship could have been the beginning of a household in which Luke would be the leader. Therefore, he needed to step up to the plate and should have clearly explained his intentions to Tracy. Just as Christ is the initiator, the man should initiate a relationship. If he did not know his intentions, then he should have backed off and let God show him what his future was to be, with or without her. When does the responsibility of the household begin? With a wedding ring? With an engagement ring? Or at the beginning of a relationship?

After an engagement followed by a marriage ceremony, the picture God is painting with a husband and wife becomes clearer. We see that the husband is to protect, lead, serve, and provide for the wife. The wife is to submit, obey and follow the guidance of her husband. When each partner lays aside personal will and replaces it with the mate's wishes, a beautiful thing takes place. I am not even sure there are words to fully express what takes place. The husband is free to bear his responsibilities and the wife is free to provide a loving environment.

I would like to point out that I am speaking of the norm. Most people would say, "But what about this or that situation." Well, God still calls a husband to be a servant leader and a wife to submit, regardless of what one's mate is doing. Belonging in this picture takes work and each one has to keep him/herself lined up with what the Father would want.

We must guard our hearts, keep them pure for the bridegroom or bride. God is the Creator of marriage, and He desires marriage to be used to honor Him. He longs for us to understand, through the path to marriage and in marriage itself, our relationship with Christ (the church and the bridegroom).

Thought Questions:
1. Why did God say, "It's not good for a man to be alone"?
2. What picture do you want to paint with your marriage? Why?
3. How do you feel about a man being the initiator?

16

Your Single Years

Enjoy your years as a single. Befriend them. Ninety percent of people walk down the aisle at least once. Rejoice in God allowing you to be single and to serve and enjoy Him distraction-free. Chances are you will be married a lot longer than you will be single. Don't waste time twiddling your thumbs and wondering when you are going to take the plunge into marriage.

Guard your emotions and protect your heart from making mistakes. Save yourself—emotionally, spiritually, and physically—for your mate. The rewards of doing so will long outlast any momentary dissatisfaction you may experience in your singleness.

Soak in all the information you can regarding what it means to be a godly man or woman. Seek the Lord with all your time, energy, money, strength. He will not return anything void.

I believe most of you picked up this book because you were looking for a solution to your dating woes. At the conclusion you may be thinking, "Well, she did give me a new way to think about this dating thing, but I am not sure it is a commitment I want to make." If you want to avoid pain in your dating relationships, then you are going to have to make a change. You can't take the same path and expect a different outcome. You must take a totally new course.

My mom always says, "A man convinced against his will is of the same persuasion still." So this must come from your heart and from the Holy Spirit convicting you. I pray that each of you, in your heart, comes to the place where God wants you.

Your new path is not always going to be easy or even fun, but we must have a renewing of our minds, hearts, and souls. If you are serious about your love relationship with the Lord, spend your single years falling in love with Him. He makes a perfect mate.

I heard a story of two angels. It is about the heart of our relationship with the all-powerful, all-knowing Father above. (I have done a little paraphrasing).

One night two angels were staying at the home of a wealthy family. This family had almost everything they wanted—spare bedrooms, extra cars, fine food. When the angels came to stay, the family did not give them a bed-room, but put them in the basement. They did not want these angels to mess up any of their fine things.

In the middle of the night the older angel woke up the younger angel with his loud tools. He was repairing a hole in the wall of the basement. This perplexed the younger angel, but he was able to drift back to sleep.

The next night they went to the home of a poor couple. Their prize possession was a cow. This cow provided their meager income.

This sweet couple gave the two angels the only comfortable spot in the house to sleep, the hay bed, while they took the floor.

The next morning they all awoke to find that the cow had died in the middle of the night. This made the younger angel very upset. In a private moment he asked the older angel, "Why did you repair the hole in the wall of the rich folks and allow the cow to die?"

The older angel replied, "Behind that hole was a great deal of gold and I did not want the rich couple to discover it. And in the middle of the night the angel of death came for the wife and I pleaded with him to take the cow."

So remember, God's way and timing will look far different than one can even imagine. He will do what is best for us, even if we struggle with understanding.

Say this prayer with me:

Father,

My life is in Your hands, You provide for me moment by moment. I ask that You open my eyes to see Your unfailing love for me and allow my stubborn heart to trust You fully. I know that I will not be single a day longer than You want me to be and in that I will find rest from this mind game of wondering and waiting. Open doors of ministry for me so that I may serve where You want me to serve. Help me protect my emotions from the pitfall of having intimacy before commitment. Continue to show me how You desire me to mirror my marriage with the marriage to Your Son. All I could want or all that could satisfy me is wrapped up in my relationship with You. Allow me to rest in You and fall more in love with You each day. In Your Son's holy and precious name, Jesus. Amen

Appendix

I want to thank you for taking time to read my book. These thoughts have been close to my heart, and writing them down has taken a few years. You may have seen glimpses of my life, but I thought I would take some time and share my testimony with you.

In 1985 my parents began homeschooling my sisters and me. I was in the sixth grade. I studied at home until 1992, when I graduated high school. My parents' philosophy was to train and raise independent, self-sufficient daughters. I knew that one day I was going to have to be out on my own, earning my keep.

I started college and began my journey as an adult. My only true heart's desire was marriage, but that did not happen. In college I began to become more and more independent, and an independent spirit grew in me. I did not need anyone and I was beginning to not even need God.

In my junior year I moved about a three-hour drive from my parents. At this time I was in an emotional relationship with a young man. We were great friends, but I always wanted more with him. We shared secrets, dreams, hopes, and past pains. Our friendship was deep and strong. We spent holidays together and our families loved the other person. All along there was nothing physical between us.

About a year into our friendship he asked me to marry him. I was a bit taken aback. We had never talked about our feelings, and this was the first time we had even talked about "us." Of course I said "Yes" and was excited.

The problem, however, was that he did not want to date. He just wanted me to wait until he was ready for marriage. This was fine at first, but then my life changed.

I wandered away from the Lord but He began drawing me back to His protective arms. My "pseudo engagement" did not fit with where I was going.

We broke off the engagement, but we never really broke up because we never really dated. Strange? Yes, it is hard to explain.

After college I moved to Denver and began working in a ministry with other people my age. I befriended a young man there. We spent time alone together, prayed together and shared things with each other. All along we were just friends. I never knew what he thought about me. Again we were never physical beyond hugging. When he moved I still never knew what he thought, but my heart hurt when he left.

When I compare the two relationships, I see that the latter affected me the most because never once did he explain himself to me one way or the other. During my year in Denver my parents presented this idea of emotional purity to my sisters and me. At first I thought it was a little strange, but then after a second heartache I was open to the idea. Their vision for us girls began to change and they saw the benefits of protecting and providing for their daughters until marriage.

This process of learning about emotional intimacy has been an awesome journey and I thank God for the men He brought in my life. All the young men in my life have taught me life lessons. Had I never experienced those relationships with those two men, I might still think I can do it on my own.

I moved home from Denver and my father's goal was to help prepare me for marriage. The process of breaking my independent spirit was interesting, but now that it has been five years, I am thankful for the freedom submission brings. It is also awesome being protected from any further heartache. My dad has taken responsibility for me and helps me from making bad choices. Most people say in their 40s, "Oh, if I had known in my 20s what I know now, my life would have been different." I have the opportunity to have my parents' 40 plus year old wisdom guiding me in decisions while in my 20's and beyond. This is freedom!

Since I have moved home and begun to prepare myself for marriage, I thank God that no man had to break me of my independent spirit. God has given my dad wisdom and grace to help me become a woman of God. Had I married before I was broken of my selfishness, it's possible I would be miserable and so would my husband.

My testimony is one of a kind, but God had to deal with me in the ways that He did. I hope that my story can help you see that I have been there and have completely changed. God can do all things! Even finish this book!

Bibliography

Chapter two:

Farris, Mike. *Dating: Training for Infidelity.* Crosswalk.com, 2000.

Chapter three:

Schlect, Christopher. *Critique of Modern Youth Ministry.* Moscow, Idaho: Canon Press, 1995.

Johnson, Erik. "Joining the Generations," *Discipleship Journal*, July/August 2000.

Chapter four:

Schlessinger, Laura. *When is an Affair an Affair?* September 11, 2000.

Chapter six:

Nikaido, Susan. "Just Friends?" *New Man*, July/August 1999.

Harris, Joshua. *I Kissed Dating Goodbye.* Sisters, Oregon: Multnomah Books, 1997.

Chapter eight:

Wakefield, Norm. *Equipped to Love Idolatry-Free Relationships.* Ashville, Alabama: Elijah Ministries, 1999.

Bibliography

Chapter nine:

Whelchel, Mary. *Common Mistakes Singles Make.* Grand Rapids, Michigan: Fleming H. Revell, 1989.

Chapter ten:

Doornenbel, Bauke and Tjitske Lemstra. *Homemaking: A Bible Study for Women at Home.* Colorado Springs, Colorado: NavPress, 1981.

Chapter twelve:

Whelchel, Mary. *Common Mistakes Singles Make.* Grand Rapids, Michigan: Fleming H. Revell, 1989.

Chapter fourteen:

Ryun, Nathaniel and Andrew. *It's a Lifestyle Discipleship in Our Relationships.* Lawrence, Kansas: Silver Clarion Press, 1996.

Chapter fifteen:

Hammond, Michelle McKinney. *The Power of Femininity Rediscovering the Art of Being a Woman.* Eugene, Oregon: Harvest House Publishers, 1999.

For speaking engagements, or if you want to share your thoughts with Heather, contact:

> Emotional Purity
> P.O. Box 264
> Lake Villa, IL 60046
>
> EmotionalPurity@aol.com

To order additional copies of

Emotional Purity
An Affair of the Heart

Have your credit card ready and call

Toll free: (877) 421-READ (7323)

or send $12.95* each plus $4.95 S & H**

to
**WinePress Publishing
PO Box 428
Enumclaw, WA 98022**

www.winepresspub.com

*Washington residents please add 8.4% tax.
**Add $1.00 S&H for each additional book ordered.

Notes

Notes

Notes

Notes

Notes

Notes

Notes

Notes

Notes

Notes

Notes